D1784037

The Derwent Valley Heritage Way

PEAK DISTRICT

Compiled by
Kevin Borman

Acknowledgements
I would like to thank Rick Jillings, Derwent Valley
Heritage Way Project Officer, whose encyclopaedic
knowledge and enthusiasm made my job easier and the
finished book more accurate. Various leaflets published
by the Derwent Valley Trust were informative and useful.
Thanks also to Ray Marjoram, of Belper Industrial
Society, and Irene Coope, of Derbyshire Wildlife Trust. In
addition, my appreciation to Pete Brown and Mick
Poulter for their pertinent suggestions after reading early
drafts of the text. Most of all, thanks to Troy Roberts as
ever for her company, humour and the use of her
binoculars.

Text:	Kevin Borman
Photography:	Kevin Borman and Jarrold Publishing
Editors:	Crawford Gillan and Sonya Calton
Designers:	Doug Whitworth and Martin Kempson

Jarrold Publishing   ISBN 0-7117-2958-1

While every care has been taken to ensure the accuracy of
the route directions, the publishers cannot accept respons-
ibility for errors or omissions, or for changes in details
given. The countryside is not static: hedges and fences can
be removed, field boundaries can alter, footpaths can be
rerouted and changes in ownership can result in the closure
or diversion of some concessionary paths. Also, paths that
are easy and pleasant for walking in fine conditions may
become slippery, muddy and difficult in wet weather, while
stepping stones across rivers and streams may become
impassable.

If you find an inaccuracy in either the text or maps,
please write or e-mail to Jarrold Publishing at the
addresses below.

First published 2003
by Jarrold Publishing

Printed in Belgium
by Proost NV, Turnhout. 1/03

Jarrold Publishing
Pathfinder Guides, Whitefriars, Norwich NR3 1JR
E-mail: info@totalwalking.co.uk
www.totalwalking.co.uk

Contents

How to use this book

 For the purposes of this guide the Derwent Valley Heritage Way has been broken into 10 separate sections, each easily enjoyed as a day's outing. The route can, of course, be done in its entirety as one long-distance walk. Either way, this guide should provide all the information you need.

To help you plan ahead, the start of each section has a brief list of the local facilities you can expect to find at places en route. This lists services such as pubs, eating places, accommodation, banks, shops and public toilets.

Incorporated in the route descriptions are areas of blue text where information about public transport can be found – allowing you to decide on the most convenient points of departure or arrival for each section.

Each part of the route has a sign to indicate the starting point for each section. The route can be seen in its entirety on the key map opposite.

Map extracts used in the book are from the 1:25,000 scale Ordnance Survey Explorer series. To view the route in a wider context you will need Explorers 1 (The Peak District – Dark Peak), 24 (The Peak District – White Peak), 259 (Derby) and 260 (Nottingham).

In addition to the information given in the route descriptions, more details about places to explore, public transport links and accommodation can be found in the Further Information section at the back of the book.

Key Map

Introduction

The Derwent Valley Heritage Way

The Derwent Valley Heritage Way is a 55-mile (88.5 km) walk that explores the beauty and heritage of Derbyshire's River Derwent. The initiative for developing this walk came from the Derwent Valley Trust (*see page 90*). Opened in 2003, the route follows the river from Ladybower Reservoir in the Peak District National Park, via Chatsworth and the superb scenery of the Derbyshire dales, before passing through the Derwent Valley Mills World Heritage Site. Taking the Riverside Path through Derby, the Way continues through the historic inland port of Shardlow to journey's end at Derwent Mouth, where the Derwent flows into the River Trent.

The Derwent Valley Heritage Way can be enjoyed either as a continuous long-distance walk or as a series of shorter outings. In this book the route description has been broken into ten sections of between 4.6 and 6.8 miles (7.2 and 11.2 km). Walking the whole route over a few days will provide a fascinating insight into the river and its many landscapes, whereas walking each section separately, at a slower pace, will give you longer to explore the valley's many attractions and points of interest.

A reasonable walking speed is about two miles an hour, excluding long stops. Thus a six-mile (10km) walk would normally take about three hours. Because there is so much of interest en route, and many teashops, pubs and shops beckoning, a six-mile walk, perhaps with a bus back to the starting point, could easily become an informative, leisurely and enjoyable day's walk. Further details of the many places to explore along the Way are provided on *page 90*. Seasoned walkers will easily manage two stages of the Way in a day but they, too, should allow time to make the most of the route.

Using the route descriptions and the 1:25,000 scale Ordnance Survey map extracts in this guide, following the Way will be easy. In addition, the route has been waymarked using small yellow and purple discs. Look out for these at road crossing points and path junctions. If you wish to see the route in a wider context, you will need the appropriate OS Explorer maps: 1 (The Peak District – Dark Peak), 24 (The Peak District – White Peak), 259 (Derby) and 260 (Nottingham). The Derwent Valley Heritage Way is to be shown on future revisions of these maps.

At the start and finish of each section of the Way there are public transport links. Frequent and reliable public transport (further details in the main text and on *page 92*) means that it is easy to walk a stretch of the Way and return by public transport. Good transport links also give you the option of leaving the car at home.

Local Tourist Information Centres (*page 93*) can provide information about accommodation – hotels, guesthouses, bed-and-breakfasts, campsites and youth hostels – available in the valley. For those wishing to explore the superb scenery of the Upper Derwent Valley to the north of the Derwent Valley

Heritage Way, information is provided on *page 93*, while details of 'Access for All' sections of the Way are on *page 95*. Those wishing to record their completion of the Way can find out how to do so on *page 95*.

The River Derwent

The River Derwent rises on Bleaklow and Howden Moors at about 2065 ft (630m) above sea level. From there it flows south for a mere 60 miles (97km) before merging with the River Trent not far south-east of Derby. The course of the Derwent lies entirely within Derbyshire, although its headwaters lie close to the Yorkshire border and its confluence with the Trent is on the Leicestershire boundary, with that of Nottinghamshire nearby.

Despite its modest length, the Derwent flows through a range of intriguing landscapes. These combine the natural beauty of stark gritstone edges and verdant valleys with an astonishing variety of man-made features. The latter range from huge dams to a stepping-stone river crossing and the vast mills where the Industrial Revolution was born, from a sublime stately house to a watchman's hut on an ancient bridge, and from a salt warehouse by a canal to a futuristic football stadium. Such is the fascinating variety of landscapes that this book will help you explore.

While walking by the Derwent you may well see herons and little grebes, and possibly kingfishers and goosanders. Parts of the valley are strongholds for water voles and bats and otters are now occasionally seen. From the angler's standpoint, upstream of Whatstandwell the Derwent is a game fishery, with trout and grayling predominating; downstream it is a coarse fishing river with chub, barbel, dace and roach.

And, of course, there is the River Derwent itself: meandering smoothly between vivid green pastures churned by slow cattle; running unnoticed alongside the occasional shabby grey factory which has turned its back on the river; foaming over neatly curved weirs and harnessed for historic mills; its banks used by industrialists, anglers, canoeists, birdwatchers, dog-walkers and, hopefully, increasing numbers of people walking the Derwent Valley Heritage Way.

In the 18th century, according to Daniel Defoe, the Derwent was 'a fury of a river'. Eighty years later William Adam called it 'a powerful and rapid stream; impetuously rushing over its rugged and broken bed.' Perhaps it was the contributions of the river's many tributaries which gave it these characteristics.

As well as receiving the River Noe at Bamford, the Derwent is joined by the Wye at Rowsley, the Amber at Ambergate and the Ecclesbourne at Duffield. Other sizeable streams lie within its catchment, too, including Peakshole Water, the Rivers Bradford and Lathkill, and the Burbage and Markeaton Brooks. The name Derwent, incidentally, is considered to mean 'river where oaks were common'.

A bewildering maze of small streams drains the moorlands of the Dark Peak

Chatsworth House

in the far north of Derbyshire, whose apt names – Bleaklow, Featherbed Moss, Rushbed Moor – indicate the wild and wet nature of the heather and bilberry-clad uplands. Thousands of tiny peat-stained runnels coalesce on the slopes of Bleaklow to create the River Derwent, and such is the extent of the catchment area on the high moors, in effect a huge sponge, that the Derwent is a substantial river within a few miles of its source.

As the Derwent has carved its course over millennia, its erosive power has been one of the key factors producing the dramatic gritstone crags, their litany of names known particularly well to climbers. Among this line of dark sandstone cliffs, mostly natural but in one or two cases enhanced by quarrying, the most famous is Stanage Edge, but the roll-call also includes Burbage, Millstone, Froggatt, Curbar, Baslow, Gardom's and Birchen Edges.

Areas of shale around Rowsley and Darley Dale have weathered to create deep soil and rich pastures that provide better agricultural possibilities and also the setting for the Chatsworth Estate. Then, a few miles farther south, the river passes into an area of limestone which adds its own dramatic features to the scene. These include the towering cliffs of Pic Tor and High Tor, below which the Derwent twists through a narrow gorge. The settlements of Matlock and Cromford mark either end of this limestone gorge with, in between them, Matlock Bath somehow managing to wedge itself into the tight defile.

South again, the Derwent flows through a picturesque but less dramatic landscape. However, in the stretch from Cromford through Belper, Milford and Darley Abbey, all the way to Derby, pioneers of the Industrial Revolution made their own remarkable impact on the valley.

Derby itself, modern and industrial, nevertheless has a Roman site. It was one of the key points of the Danelaw, and it is a county town and cathedral city. Neither does the story end at Derby. In its lower reaches, the Derwent passes parks, weirs, and modern redevelopments at Pride Park before finally coming to Shardlow, a surprisingly well-preserved inland port. Just beyond Shardlow, at an unusual triple confluence, the Trent and Mersey Canal, the Derwent and the Trent all meet.

From here the Trent heads north-east through Nottingham and Newark-on-Trent before veering north via Gainsborough. Some 60 miles from the Derwent-Trent confluence, the Trent meets the Ouse, near Alkborough, to form the River Humber. Already hugely wide at this point, the Humber then flows east for some 35 miles (56km) to empty itself into the North Sea at Spurn Head. It's hard to imagine, as you walk by the dipper-haunted waters of the Derwent below the brooding or sunlit facets of Millstone Edge, that this same water, in a few days' time, will have been swallowed up, somewhere beyond Cleethorpes, in the endless grey realms of the North Sea.

Reservoirs and Country Estates
The River Derwent has had to endure a remarkable amount of human intrusion, some of it bad but the majority, perhaps surprisingly, positive.

In the first half of the 20th century water engineers, recognising the extent and reliability of the rainfall on the Peak District moors, created a chain of three reservoirs in the Upper Derwent Valley. The Derwent Valley Water Board was set up in 1899 and within 20 years the Howden and Derwent reservoirs had been created. Ladybower Reservoir, the largest of the three, was a later addition, being completed in the 1940s.

Not only water engineers but also landowners and their talented employees saw the potential of the Derwent Valley. Chatsworth, one of England's most celebrated estates, lies between Baslow and Rowsley. The present Chatsworth House was built in the late 17th century at the bidding of the fourth Earl (later the first Duke) of Devonshire. The1000-acre (405ha) park on the banks of the Derwent is open all year. There is a 105-acre (42ha) garden which incorporates a maze, rose, cottage and kitchen gardens and the first Duke's water cascade and the Emperor Fountain. Outside again, to mark the 200th anniversary of the birth of Joseph

Trees in autumn alongside the River Derwent at Leadmill Bridge

Paxton, head gardener from 1826 to 1858, his monumental rock garden has been fully restored for 2003. A sensory garden is a new addition designed to stimulate the eyes and the nostrils. Elisabeth Frink's sculpture, *Walking Madonna*, is a recent purchase.

A little farther off-route, but worth a visit, lies Haddon Hall, a splendid medieval and Tudor manor house on the A6 between Bakewell and Rowsley.

The Derwent Valley Mills World Heritage Site

The River Derwent has attracted industry for centuries. Lead was mined in Derbyshire before Roman times. There is a record of nail-making in Belper as far back as 1313, and by 1566 Hathersage had a wire-making works.

The real concentration of industry, however, was along the 15 miles (24km) of river that snakes from Matlock Bath to Derby. Here is found a fascinating series of historic mill complexes, including some of the world's first 'modern' factories. No less important are the watercourses that powered them, the settlements that were built for the mill workers, and the remains of one of the world's earliest long distance railways, all in the context of a landscape that has changed little over two centuries.

In December 2001, the Derwent Valley between Matlock Bath and Derby was designated by UNESCO as a cultural World Heritage Site, one of only 21 such sites in mainland Britain. The citation states: 'The cultural landscape of the Derwent Valley is of outstanding significance because it was here that the modern factory system was established to accommodate the new technology for spinning cotton developed by Richard Arkwright. The insertion of industrial establishments into a rural landscape necessitated the construction of housing for the workers in the mills, and the resulting settlements created an exceptional industrial landscape that has retained its qualities over two centuries.'

Sir Richard Arkwright's magnificent Masson Mills at Matlock Bath stand at the northern entrance to the World Heritage Site. Established in 1783, and in continuous use until 1991, the mills now house a working textile museum and a modern retail village. The museum's clatter of well-oiled machinery and the whirr of drive-belts takes the visitor back to a time when generations of local millworkers trod the wooden floors.

A short distance south of Masson Mills lies Arkwright's Cromford Mill, the world's first successful water-powered cotton spinning mill. Building began here in 1771 and the complex, which contains an exhibition, restaurant and shops, is, at the time of writing, undergoing painstaking restoration.

As water-power was harnessed to move the cotton industry out of homes and into purpose-built factories the village of Cromford, where most of Arkwright's workforce lived, grew up close to his mills.

In transport terms, the remains of significant features can be seen along the Cromford Canal and at the High Peak Junction workshops.

Riber Castle from High Tor

At the northern edge of Belper stands William Strutt's North Mill of 1804. Built using pioneering 'fire proof' technology, the mill now houses the Derwent Valley Visitor Centre and an interpretative museum that provides a stimulating insight into the lives of those who worked in the Strutt family mills.

Downstream again, beyond the mill village of Milford and on the northern edge of Derby, lies the community of Darley Abbey. Here, water power was already in use driving paper, corn, flint and leather mills when, in 1782, the Evans family added their Boar's Head Cotton Mills and later their factory village.

From here a walk through Darley Park leads to Derby Industrial Museum, which marks the southern entrance to the World Heritage Site. Built on the site of John Lombe's Silk Mill of the early 1720s, England's first 'modern' factory, the museum illustrates Derbyshire's abundant industrial legacy.

Beyond the southern reaches of the World Heritage Site the historical interest continues, most notably at Shardlow, an inland river port with a Heritage Centre to tell the full story. The impact of industry on the Derwent Valley was such that, by the end of the 19th century, it was turning out an astonishing variety of products: lace and candles, paint and boots, telescopes and hats, cheese and pearl buttons.

Walking the valley now, what is striking is not simply the amount of industrial history it contains but also the fact that it is, for all this development, still remarkably rural and scenically impressive. ■

1 SECTION ONE

Heatherdene to Leadmill Bridge (Hathersage)

START Heatherdene
FINISH Leadmill Bridge/Hathersage
DISTANCE 5.2 miles (8.4km)/5.7 miles (9.4km)
TERRAIN Easy walking, mainly on a disused railway and field paths

PUBLIC TRANSPORT

To the start at Heatherdene, buses from Sheffield and from Bamford station on the Sheffield – Manchester line. From the finish at Hathersage, buses to Sheffield, Chesterfield and Bakewell; trains to Sheffield and Manchester

FACILITIES EN ROUTE

Bamford

Pubs, B&Bs/guesthouses, shop, PO, recreation ground, caravan site

Hathersage

Wide range of facilities including pubs and eating places, accommodation, shops, banks, outdoor equipment supplier

Hathersage has a heated outdoor swimming pool. Nearest campsite is at North Lees and a youth hostel is on the edge of the village

Heatherdene **1**

Leadmill Bridge **2**

Baslow **3**

Rowsley **4**

Matlock **5**

Whatstandwell **6**

Belper **7**

Little Eaton **8**

Derby City Centre **9**

Borrowash Bridge **10**

Derwent Mouth

DERWENT VALLEY HERITAGE WAY

Hathersage

The first stretch of the Way begins alongside Ladybower Reservoir and follows the line of a dismantled railway southwards between the heights of Win Hill and Bamford Edge, before taking to the riverbank for a stroll through meadows to Leadmill Bridge, near Hathersage.

The route crosses Ladybower Dam, providing fine views of Ladybower Tor, continues to a millennium sculpture trail and then carries on to Hathersage where the churchyard is said to be the final resting place of Robin Hood's lieutenant Little John. Charlotte Bronte stayed at the nearby vicarage in 1845.

Heatherdene to Leadmill Bridge

From Heatherdene car park, take the surfaced path south for 400 yds (365m) past occasional picnic tables. Through the narrow belt of trees you can glimpse Ladybower Reservoir with its many-arched viaduct carrying the A57, and the unusual double top of Crook Hill rising to the north-west.

A Just beyond an information board bear right, descend the steps and cross the A6013. A permissive path now allows passage across the dam. Looking north from the dam, although most of Ladybower Reservoir is hidden due to a dog-leg, there is a fine view of Ladybower Tor while, to the south, the Derwent Valley is largely clothed in deciduous woodland.

B At the western end of the dam is one of the Bamford parish

■ Ladybower Dam, the last of the three dams to be built in the Upper Derwent Valley, was constructed between 1935-39 and officially opened in 1945, to supply water to Sheffield, Nottingham, Leicester and Derby. Quite recently, extensive work was undertaken to reinforce the ageing structure. Between September 1998 and December 1999, 400,000 tonnes of sandstone were taken from Win Hill. The work was suspended between January and June 1999 to avoid disturbing nesting herons and goshawks. The slopes of Win Hill were reinstated when quarrying was complete. As part of the renovation scheme, a permissive path, now used by the Derwent Valley Heritage Way, was created across the top of the dam.

Touchstones, part of a sculpture trail established by the villagers to mark the millennium. This sculpture has a

Fishing on Ladybower Reservoir

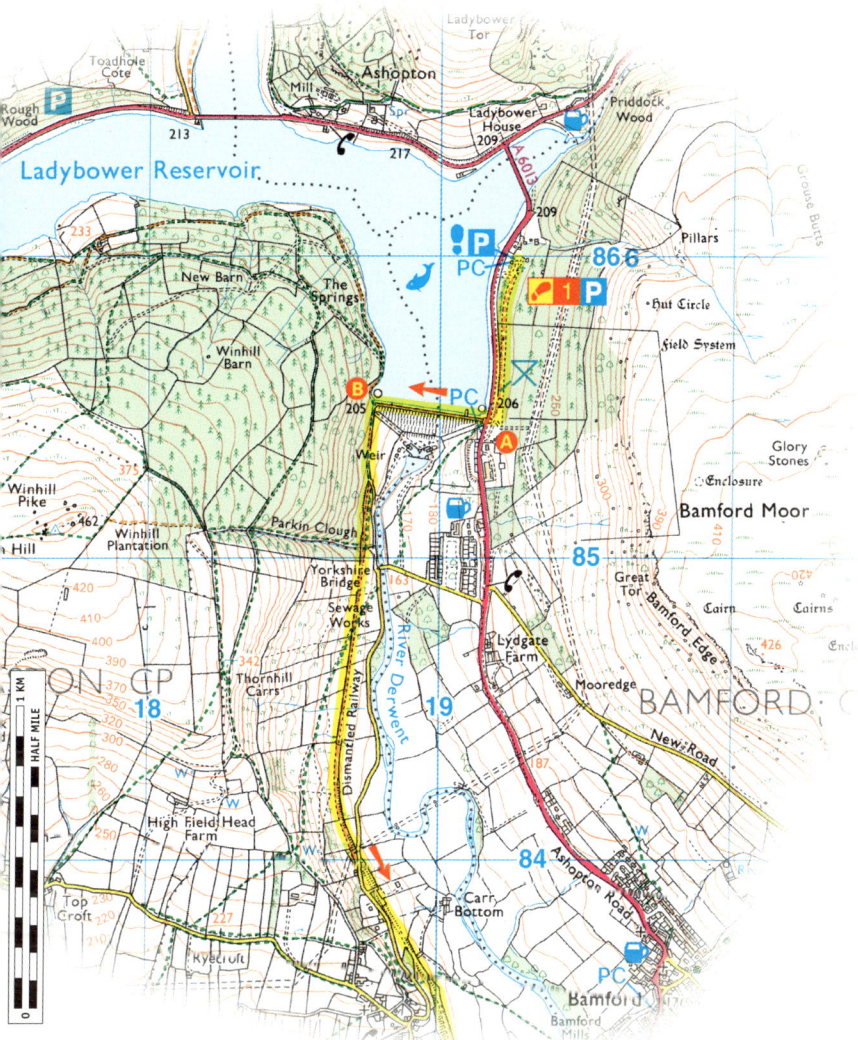

'water' theme. Turn left, downhill, on a surfaced track by a wall. After about 275 yds (250m) take an obvious track branching off on the right. This, now known as the Thornhill Trail, is the line of the old railway that was built to bring the stone for the building of the dam.

On reaching a minor road, cross it with a small zigzag by some wooden stakes and continue south on the line of the old railway. There are good views across to the craggy crest of

The regimented rows of houses that form Yorkshire Bridge, just south of Ladybower Dam, were built to rehouse residents of Ashopton and Derwent, two villages drowned when Ladybower Reservoir was filled. The village has a pub of the same name, but downhill from the village, and spanning the River Derwent, is Yorkshire Bridge itself. This despite the fact that the county boundary between Derbyshire and Yorkshire is more than two miles away to the north-east.

Stepping stones across the River Derwent

Bamford Edge as you pass a further Touchstone, with an 'earth' theme. Beyond this, the houses of Bamford are visible across the valley to your left.

C When you reach Water Lane, turn left. In less than 100 yds (91m), the building on the left with a large stone inscription DERWENT VALLEY WATER BOARD was once the headquarters of that body. It has recently been converted into sheltered accommodation. Opposite this take a stile on the right. Follow the field edge on your right to curve round and pass underneath the railway. Continue ahead across a gravelled area, with a garden centre off to your left, to reach a gate and the A6187.

➤ ▭ ▯ Bamford station and a bus stop are only a few minutes walk away. Follow the Hathersage direction and walk over Mytham Bridge. The bus stop is at the toll gate. For the station, walk towards Bamford and you will soon see the sign to it.

D Cross the busy A6187 with care and, virtually opposite, take Shatton Lane which bridges the River Noe. Just beyond the bridge, take the stile on the left. A few yards farther on cross a narrow footbridge and climb the riverbank. Close by, the River Noe flows into the Derwent. The Way now continues south-east along the bank of the river with, in the distance, Millstone Edge lying high on the horizon.

E Beyond Kentney Barn, a substantial stone affair, you soon reach a track which veers off to the right. Ignore this and continue along the riverbank. Cross another footbridge and go briefly along the top of a river bluff before coming alongside the river again.

A line of stepping-stones crosses the

■ **1 6** ■

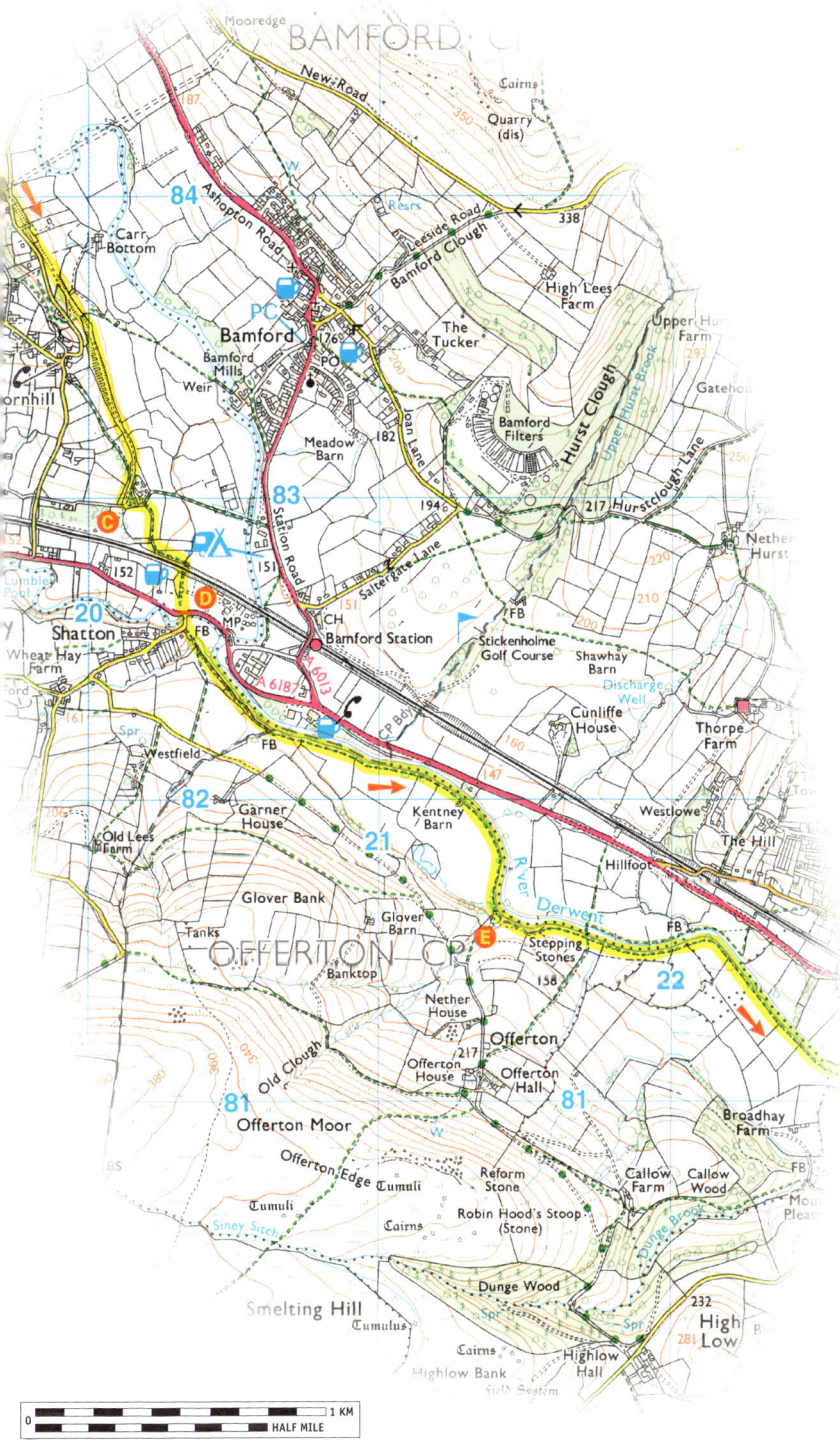

Millstone Edge from Leadmill Bridge

river just beyond here. They are quite photogenic when the river is in spate and fortunately our route does not use them. A little farther on, a low wire fence confines the path close to the river, and with a drop of about ten feet, you need to watch your footing.

After another footbridge the path enters Goose Nest Wood before opening out again for the final section to Leadmill Bridge. It's worth scanning the river here as dippers and grey wagtails can often be seen. Look downstream and you will also see, rearing up to form the skyline,

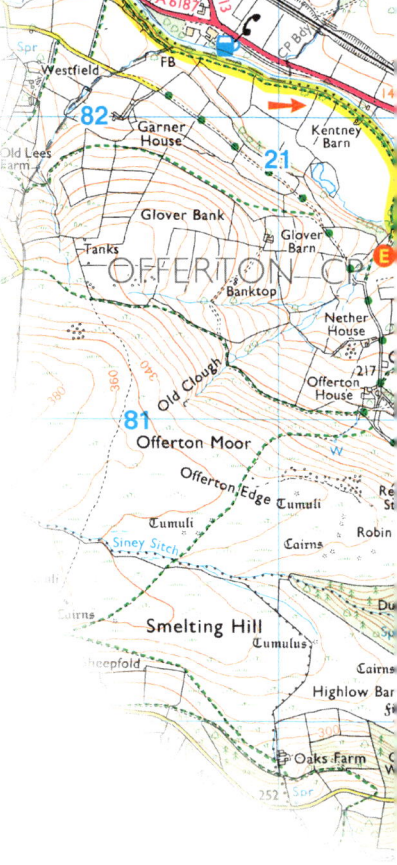

■ A grave 10 ft (3m) long in Hathersage churchyard is reputedly the resting place of Robin Hood's lieutenant Little John. In 1845 Charlotte Bronte stayed at the vicarage next to the churchyard and, in her novel *Jane Eyre*, based the village of Morton on Hathersage. Just south of the village lies the unusual round factory of cutlery designer David Mellor.

the quarried profile of Millstone Edge. To the right is the Plough Inn, while Hathersage lies less than half a mile (804m) to the left.

F ⇌ 🚌 **P** To reach Hathersage for accommodation, or for bus or train connections, continue over Leadmill Bridge towards Hathersage then, in a few yards, take a footpath on the left that follows the edges of fields to a stone stile by a lodge. For a direct route to the village centre, follow the minor road to the left. For Hathersage station, turn right along Dore Lane. At the T-junction, the station approach is opposite, half-right. ◼

Leadmill Bridge to Baslow

START	**Leadmill Bridge/Hathersage**
FINISH	**Baslow**
DISTANCE	**6.8 miles (11.2km)/7.4 miles (12.2km)**
TERRAIN	**Tracks and paths by riverside and through woods and fields**

PUBLIC TRANSPORT

To the start at Hathersage, buses from Sheffield, Chesterfield and Bakewell; trains from Sheffield and Manchester. Trains from Grindleford station to Sheffield and Manchester. Buses from Calver Bridge and the finish at Baslow to Sheffield, Manchester, Chesterfield and Matlock

FACILITIES EN ROUTE

Grindleford
Pub, hotel, B&B/guesthouse, shop, PO, recreation ground

Calver
Pubs, B&Bs/guesthouses, café, outdoor equipment supplier, PO, campsite

Baslow
B&B/guesthouse, hotel, pubs and tearooms, outdoor equipment supplier

Heatherdene — 1
Leadmill Bridge — 2
Baslow — 3
Rowsley — 4
Matlock — 5
Whatstandwell — 6
Belper — 7
Little Eaton — 8
Derby City Centre — 9
Borrowash Bridge — 10
Derwent Mouth

Baslow Edge

For much of this section the Way follows the Derwent closely. As well as ancient woodland and fine old bridges, there are distant views of the gritstone edges and close-ups of buildings as varied as Calver Mill and Bubnell Hall.

Calver Mill is an impressive building and was once used as a screen set for the television series *Colditz*. When you reach Bridge End, the oldest part of Baslow, galleries and refreshments offer a welcome taste of civilisation.

SECTION TWO

Leadmill Bridge to Baslow

≷ 🚌 🅿 To reach Leadmill Bridge from Hathersage village centre take the B6001 for 440 yds (400m) as far as Dore Lane on your right. From Hathersage railway station walk up Station Approach to reach the same point. Go along Dore Lane as far as the lodge. Here, take the stone stile on the left and follow a path along field edges to Leadmill Bridge.

Just north of Leadmill Bridge turn east and take the footpath which follows a surfaced private track to Harper Lees. Watch out for occasional carved stones stranded in the grass by the track. They seem like the remains of an exotic villa but were, in fact, salvaged from a large steel plant in South Yorkshire.

🅰 At the cattle-grid immediately before Harper Lees, take a few steps right and follow the footpath ahead as signposted, across a meadow. The path soon regains the riverbank by a redundant stile made from a railway sleeper. The ground slopes up to the left here, with a mixture of rushy pasture, dark drystone walls and broadleaved trees.

🅱 At a small gate, the Way enters Coppice Wood, part of the National Trust's Longshaw Estate.

≷ 🚌 🅿 Link to Grindleford Station 0.9 mile (1.4km): After 100 yards (91m), a few paces beyond a

> ■ Leadmill Bridge, originally known as Hazelford Bridge, was built in the 18th century for the use of packhorse trains. It had its original arches widened both up and downstream in 1928.

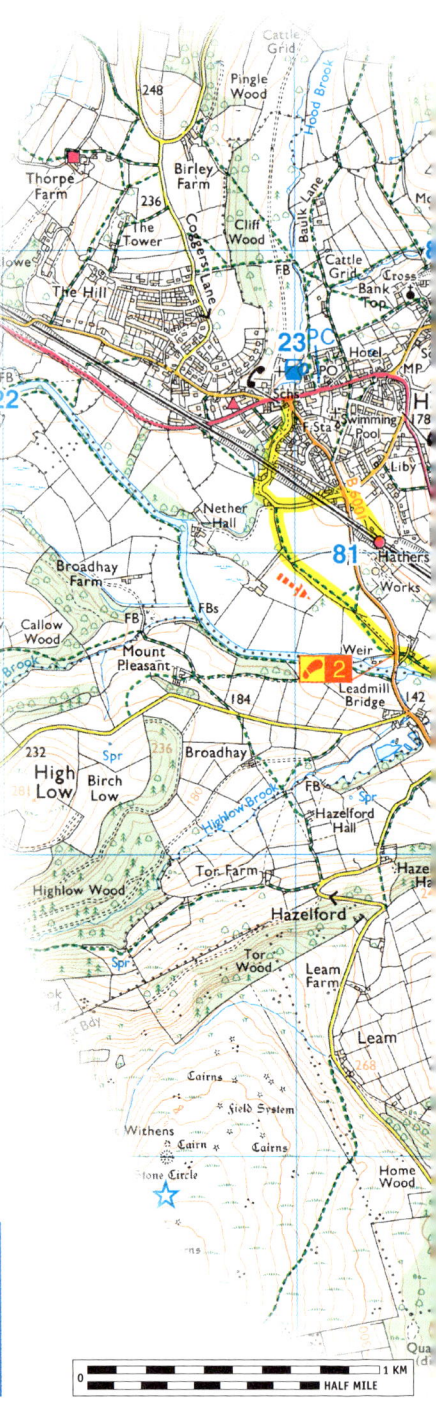

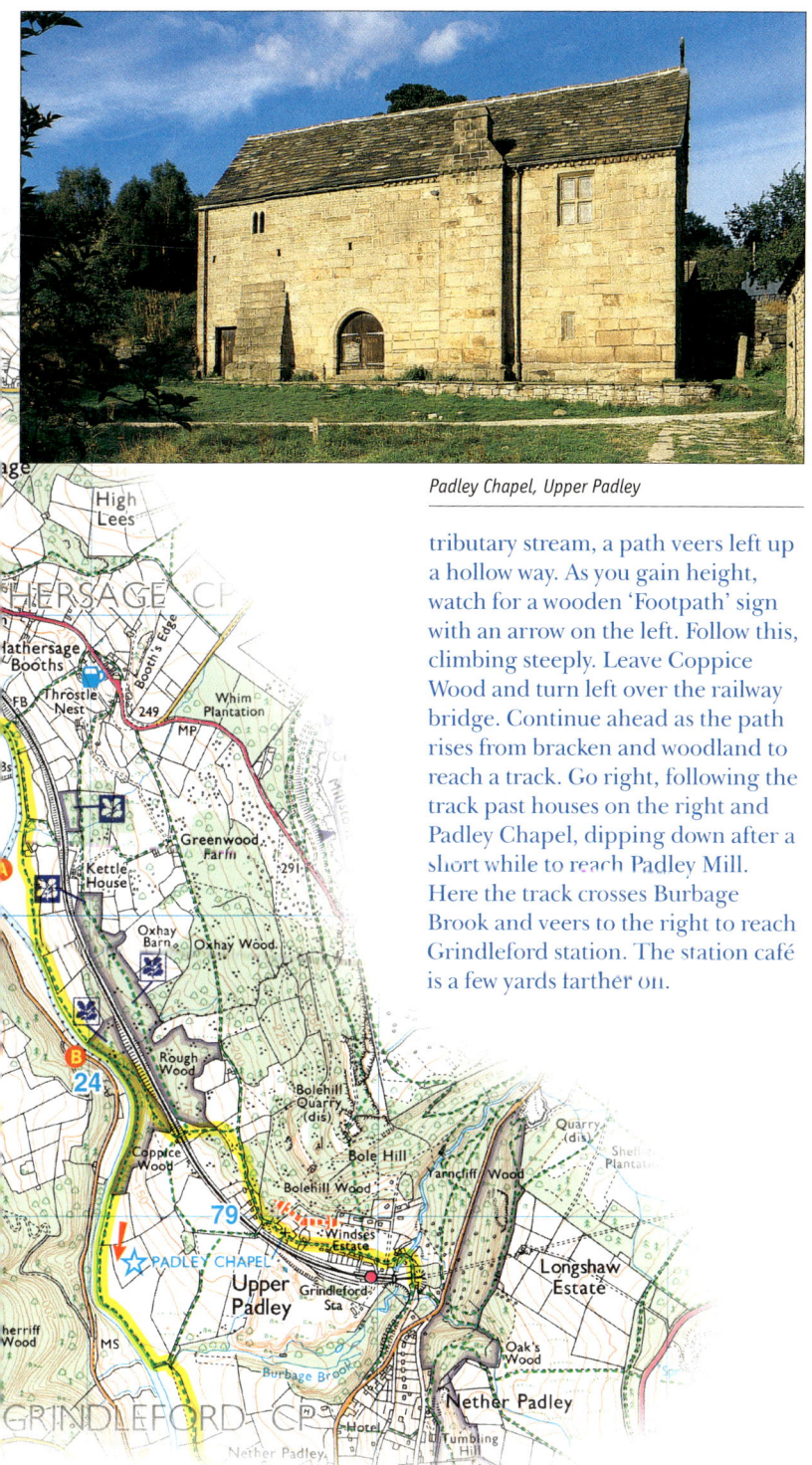

Padley Chapel, Upper Padley

tributary stream, a path veers left up a hollow way. As you gain height, watch for a wooden 'Footpath' sign with an arrow on the left. Follow this, climbing steeply. Leave Coppice Wood and turn left over the railway bridge. Continue ahead as the path rises from bracken and woodland to reach a track. Go right, following the track past houses on the right and Padley Chapel, dipping down after a short while to reach Padley Mill. Here the track crosses Burbage Brook and veers to the right to reach Grindleford station. The station café is a few yards farther on.

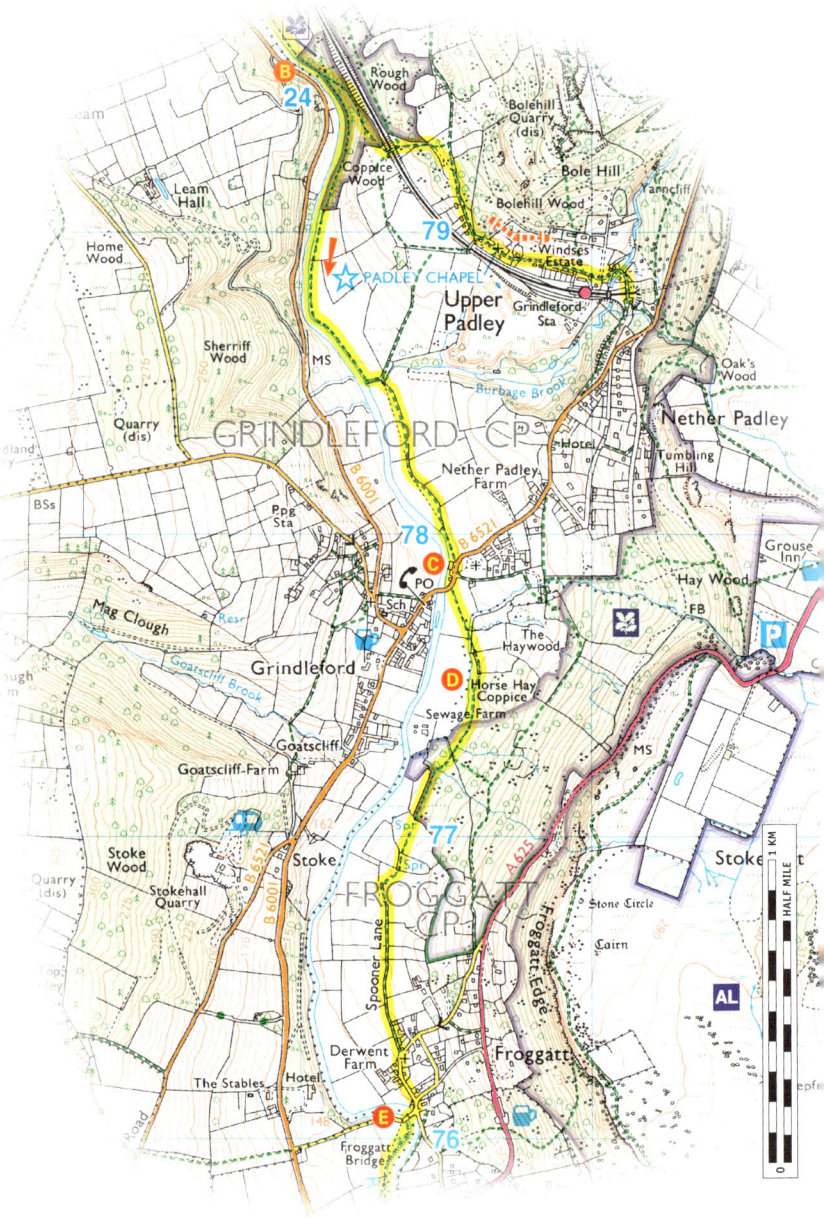

Continue along the river bank. Mallards seem particularly frequent along here. After the Way leaves Coppice Wood, to the left there are views of Tumbling Hill and Froggatt Edge. Along the river are several weirs in various states of disrepair, an indication of its historical importance for fishing. The path takes a concrete bridge over Burbage Brook, a substantial tributary of the Derwent, and continues ahead towards Grindleford.

C On reaching the B6521, cross immediately then go right for 50 yds

(46m) to a gate by an ornate cast-iron sign provided by the Peak and Northern Footpath Preservation Society, which announces that you are 427 ft (130m) above sea level. The path now heads diagonally across a field, away from the river.

D Climbing slightly, the path enters Horse Hay Coppice, another National Trust landholding, where the path is surfaced in places with gritstone setts. At a pair of stone uprights, the name changes to Froggatt Wood and the path weaves on among moss-covered boulders and deciduous trees. At a squeeze-stile the path leaves the woodland and takes to the fields.

It veers to the right of a wall near a stone barn and continues as a cobbled way. Beyond a metal gate this runs between drystone walls to reach Spooner Lane and enter Froggatt. Glance to the right for views of Stoke Hall and continue along Hollowgate to Froggatt Bridge.

■ The link route to Grindleford station passes Padley Chapel where, in the unenlightened times of Elizabeth I, a raid by the Lord Lieutenant of Derbyshire led to the arrest of two Catholic priests, Robert Ludlam and Nicholas Garlic, who were subsequently hanged, drawn and quartered at Derby.

E Cross the hefty stone bridge which provides good views both ways along the river and after a stile, follow the path on the west bank through larches. This is usually a good stretch for birdwatchers. There are coots and moorhens and sometimes, in winter, tufted ducks and goosanders.

After a swampy area with rushes and alders the path veers right to a footbridge over Stoke Brook, then left to the road at New Bridge. There is an awkward bend right by the bridge but it's worth taking in the view east from the bridge over the vast pool in the river created by a

On Froggatt Edge, above Grindleford

The watchman's guard house by the Old Bridge, Bridge End, Baslow

massive weir a little way downstream. *Take care, however, as there is often heavy traffic.*

F From New Bridge, take the track along the south bank. Once past the cottages, you will see a broad mill race on the left and, through the trees, the curved white fall of the enormous weir. The Way then angles across a field to enter a small caravan site at Stocking Farm. The buildings

---

■ By the Old Bridge (1603) at Bridge End, the oldest part of Baslow, is a tiny watchman's guard house, reputedly used to prevent the entry of undesirables into the village. Nearby is St Anne's Church, with a clock face commemorating a Diamond Jubilee. The legend VICTORIA 1897 is used in place of the numerals.

Nether End, the newer part of Baslow, grew up at the edge of Chatsworth Park during the 19th century when hotels were built to accommodate the park's visitors.

---

here include a fine stone barn, once used for parish services, with mullioned windows and external steps supported by columns, and an adjacent cottage with a curved end wall. Soon the vast bulk of Calver Mill rears up on the left. Beyond this the Way emerges at a small general store alongside Calver Bridge.

G Go left for a few yards then right, to use the underpass below the A623. Beyond a few houses, the Way continues through fields on the Derwent's west bank. The path enters St. Mary's Wood by a wide, tranquil bend in the river and follows the inside edge of the wood by a mossy wall. Leaving the wood at a wall stile, the Way follows a sometimes muddy path. Away to the east is the dark, craggy skyline of Baslow Edge.

Just before the track reaches a gate, go left through a stile and cross a field to Townend Wood. Here you reach a roughly surfaced track which is actually a minor road, Bubnell Lane. After a short way its surface changes to tarmac and it passes the splendid Bubnell Hall, thought to be the oldest house in the parish and once a school. Meanwhile, on the Derwent there is a long, steep weir and the houses of Bridge End with their river frontage.

H Cross the bridge, pausing for the views, and you are in Bridge End, where refreshments and galleries offer a taste of civilisation. Cross the road, turn right to follow Church Street briefly then bear left along School Lane, gradually gaining height to a small, triangular green with two benches. Here, take Eaton Lane, losing the height you have just gained, to reach Goose Green at Nether End. ■

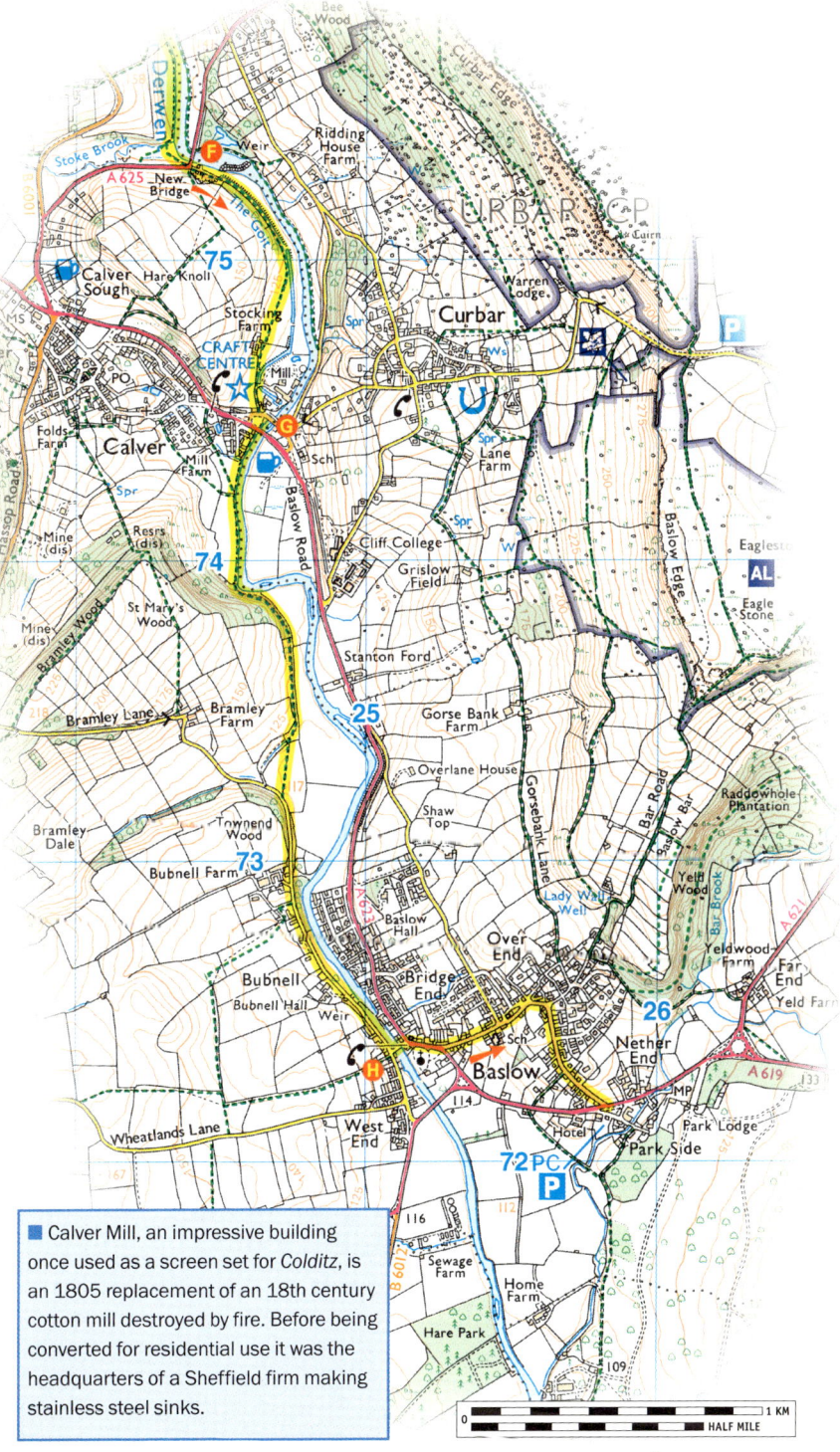

■ Calver Mill, an impressive building once used as a screen set for *Colditz*, is an 1805 replacement of an 18th century cotton mill destroyed by fire. Before being converted for residential use it was the headquarters of a Sheffield firm making stainless steel sinks.

0   1 KM
HALF MILE

SECTION THREE

Baslow to Rowsley

START	**Baslow**
FINISH	**Rowsley**
DISTANCE	**4.6 miles (7.4km)**
TERRAIN	**Tracks and paths, sometimes muddy in places**

PUBLIC TRANSPORT

To the start at Baslow, buses from Sheffield, Manchester, Chesterfield and Matlock. From the finish at Rowsley, buses to Manchester, Sheffield, Matlock, Derby and Nottingham

FACILITIES EN ROUTE

Rowsley
Pubs, hotel, B&Bs/guesthouses, shops

Beeley
Pub

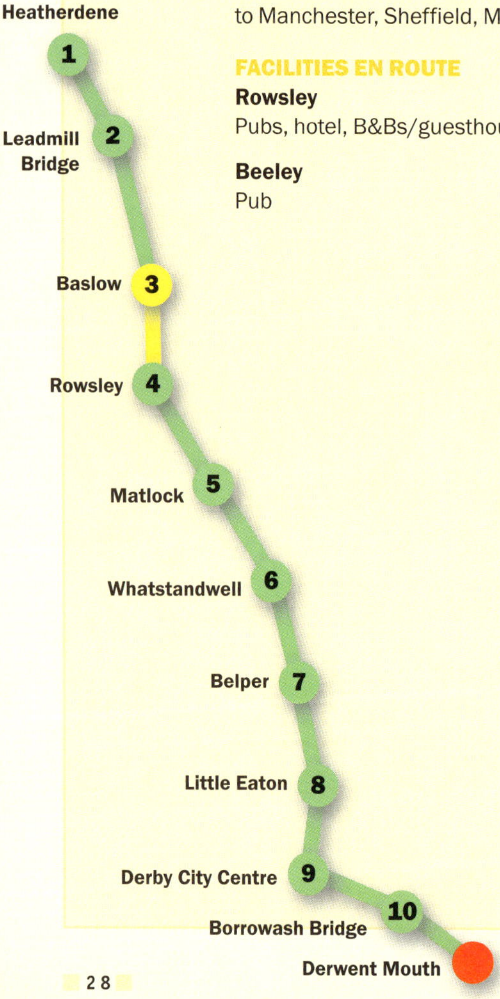

Heatherdene
1

Leadmill
Bridge
2

Baslow
3

Rowsley
4

Matlock
5

Whatstandwell
6

Belper
7

Little Eaton
8

Derby City Centre
9

Borrowash Bridge
10

Derwent Mouth

Chatsworth House beyond the Derwent

The highlight of this short section of the Way is the impressive Chatsworth Estate, with its house set in an extensive deer park landscaped by Lancelot (Capability) Brown. The Emperor Fountain, which sends up a 290ft (88m) jet of water, is one of the park's striking features. Both the grounds and the house itself, which contains superb examples of art and craftsmanship, deserve prolonged exploration. As the route winds through the estate south to Rowsley, there are close views of the Derwent.

At the end of this section Caudwell's Mill, a 19th-century grade II-listed roller flour mill with pre-1914 machinery powered by two water turbines, is also well worth a visit. The displays and hands-on models make it particularly child-friendly and there are several craft outlets as well as a shop selling different types of flour.

SECTION THREE

Baslow to Rowsley

From the village green in Baslow, take the lane to the right of the Goose Green tearooms. Go over the bridge then turn sharp right past the thatched cottages to reach The Cannon Kissing-Gate. This cleverly designed gate, which gives access to Chatsworth Park for visitors in wheelchairs, was inspired by Mrs Jill Cannon and opened in March 1999.

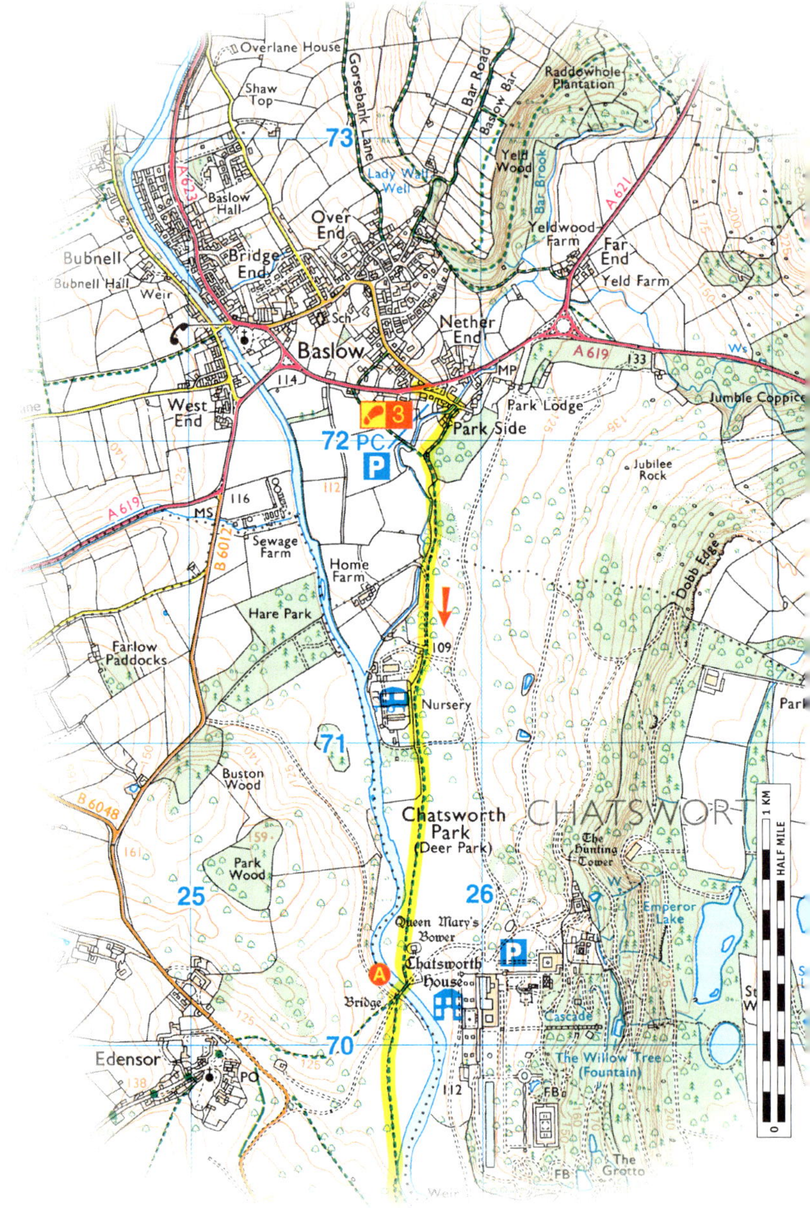

Continue ahead on the obvious path, passing White Lodge. By the time you reach the end of a wall on the right, with a cricket field beyond, Chatsworth House is visible ahead to the left.

Ⓐ Shortly you reach Queen Mary's Bower. Mary Queen of Scots was at Chatsworth five times between 1570 and 1581 whilst in custody, and this summer-house may have been built for her. Just beyond the bower, take the bridge over the Derwent.

Turn south from the bridge, crossing the meadows at a tangent, although if you prefer you can follow the river-bank as this area has open access for

■ Sir William and Lady Cavendish, known as 'Bess of Hardwick', had the original Chatsworth House built. All that remains from this period is the Hunting Tower among the trees on the high ground behind the house. The present Chatsworth House is the second on the site. It was built between 1685 and 1707 at the instigation of the fourth Earl of Devonshire who, in 1694, became the first Duke of Devonshire. Chatsworth is very much a house of local materials with its gritstone, grey marble and blackstone all coming from nearby quarries. Both the grounds and the house itself, which contains superb art and craftsmanship, are worthy of prolonged exploration.

Fallow deer in Chatsworth Park

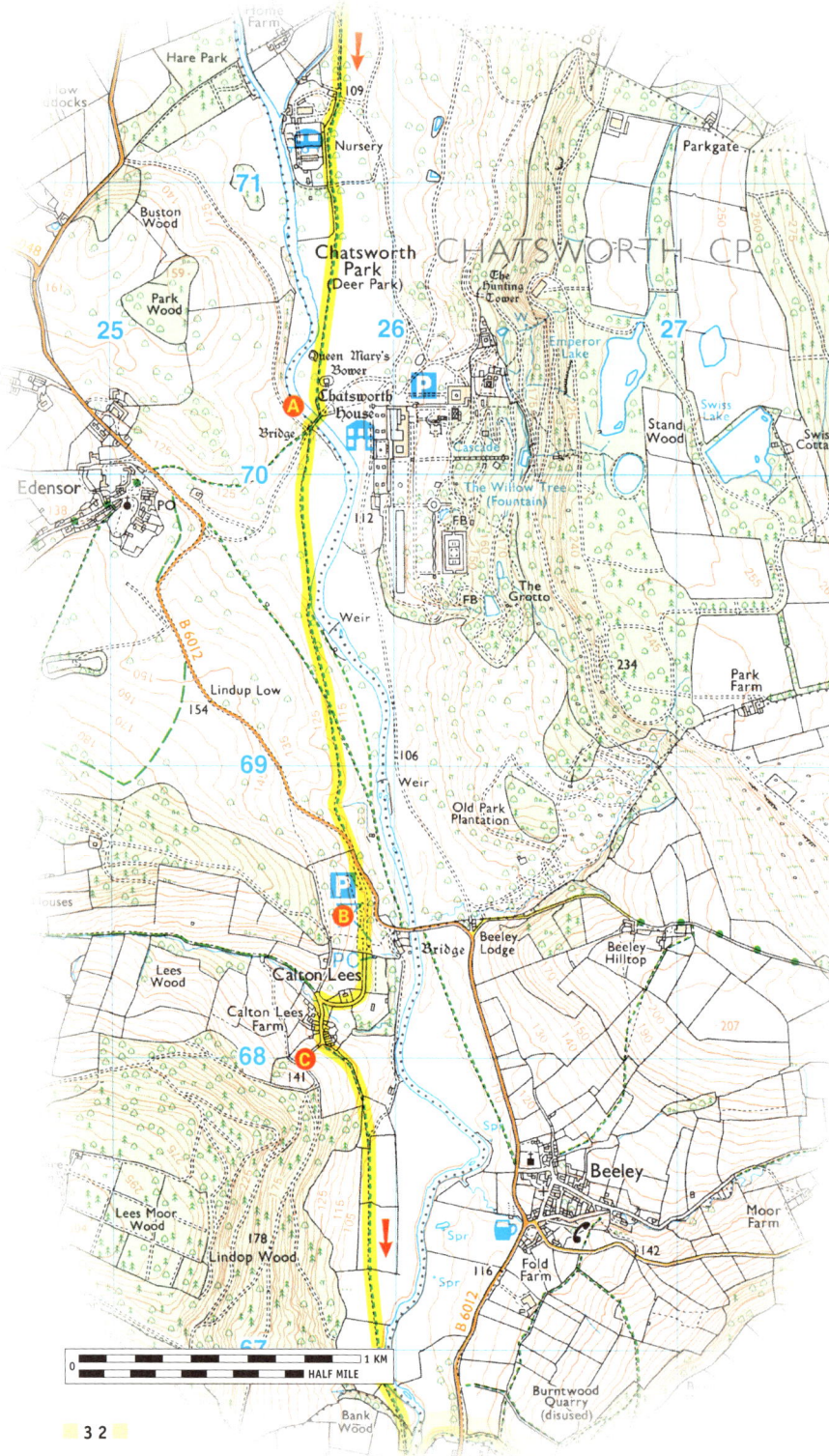

■ The landscaping of Chatsworth was the initiative of the fourth Duke of Devonshire (1720 – 1764). He employed Lancelot (Capability) Brown to create his park, at what was then the western edge of Sherwood Forest. The Emperor Fountain, which sends up a 290 ft (88m) jet of water, was the work of Sir Joseph Paxton and the sixth Duke. (Further information about Chatsworth appears in the 'Reservoirs and Country Estates' section of the Introduction.)

walking and picnicking. There are fine views across to the frontage of Chatsworth House.

On reaching a river bend by a small group of beeches, where the path is muddy, climb the river bluff to a series of benches dated 2000 and inscribed with people's Millennium Resolutions.

Continue along the top edge of the river terrace, which is marked by occasional trees with the Derwent a little way off on the left. Soon there is a weir with rapids below it and picnic tables on the near bank. Just after this, cross a tiny stream to the right of the ruined corn mill. Built during the 18th century, this mill worked until 1952 but was destroyed when three beech trees were blown onto it during gales in 1962. The Way reaches the road at a white gate by a cattle-grid just above the old mill.

B Continue ahead through the car park. The Way goes straight on from the car park, although on the left there is a possible out-and-back diversion via a short track, down to a garden centre and tearoom. The lane from the car park curves right by a saw mill. About 200 yds (182m) beyond, the quiet road makes a dog-leg to the left to pass through the hamlet of Calton Lees with its houses of rich, honey-coloured stone. By the last buildings the tarmac ends.

C At a stile, a signpost indicates Rowsley. Across the Derwent Valley lies Beeley, a small, nucleated village hunkering below the dark upper

The Derwent Valley Heritage Way passing through the hamlet of Calton Lees

Sunset, Peak Tor, near Rowsley

slopes of Beeley Moor. The path, often muddy, particularly where cattle have funnelled through gateways, dips and continues south. It passes briefly through Bank Wood and, not far beyond this, becomes a track which wends its way towards Rowsley. Along this stretch, the River Derwent forms the eastern boundary of the Peak District National Park. On passing under a disused railway bridge and reaching a village street, turn left and soon you are at the A6.

D Glance up and half right to note the tree-clad cone of Peak Tor, before turning left across the front of the Peacock Hotel. The date 1652 carved in stone above the door of this fine building marks its construction by John Stevenson, agent of the Manners family of nearby Haddon Hall. Opposite is the entrance to Caudwell's Mill, where there is now a craft centre, industrial museum and café.

Continue on the footway beside the A6, crossing the Derwent and passing The Grouse and Claret, which has its own caravan park. Behind this, and accessed from Chatsworth Road, is a large modern retail village. ■

■ The present Caudwell's Mill was built in 1874 by John Caudwell on a site where there has been a mill for at least 400 years, and was run as a family business for over a century. It is a grade II-listed roller flour mill with mostly pre-1914 machinery, powered by two water turbines. There are displays, descriptions and hands-on models throughout the mill, providing a particularly informative visit for those with children, together with several craft outlets in the Stable Yard. A variety of flour types are on sale in the mill shop.

SECTION FOUR
Rowsley to Matlock

START	**Rowsley**
FINISH	**Matlock**
DISTANCE	**5.2 miles (8.4km)**
TERRAIN	**Tracks, paths and minor roads. Occasionally muddy in places**

PUBLIC TRANSPORT

To the start at Rowsley, buses from Manchester, Sheffield, Matlock, Derby and Nottingham. Peak Rail between Rowsley South and Matlock Riverside. From the finish at Matlock, buses to Manchester, Buxton, Sheffield, Chesterfield, Nottingham and Derby; trains to Derby, Burton-on-Trent and Birmingham

FACILITIES EN ROUTE
Darley Dale
Wide range of facilities including pubs and eating places, hotels and guesthouses/B&Bs, shops, PO, bank, caravan park

Matlock
All facilities, including swimming pool and youth hostel

Heatherdene 1

Leadmill Bridge 2

Baslow 3

Rowsley 4

Matlock 5

Whatstandwell 6

Belper 7

Little Eaton 8

Derby City Centre 9

Borrowash Bridge 10

Derwent Mouth

DERWENT VALLEY HERITAGE WAY

Matlock

From Rowsley the Way follows the Derwent closely at first then visits the quiet, attractive settlements of Churchtown, Darley Bridge and Oker before again running alongside the river to enter Matlock, the first sizeable town on the route.

Near the start of this section a steam railway is operated by the Peak Railways Heritage Trust and there are also exhibitions, shops and refreshments. The high ground of Stanton Moor, with its stone circles and Bronze Age burial mounds, is worthy of exploration while St Helen's churchyard at Churchtown has a 1,000-year-old yew tree.

SECTION FOUR

Rowsley to Matlock

A few yards west of the sharp bend in Rowsley, where Chatsworth Road joins the A6, is Old Station Close. Follow this to its end where a concessionary footpath is signposted 'Riverside path to Northwood'. This takes a strip of woodland along the east bank of the Derwent. After a short way the Derwent receives one of its major tributaries, the Wye, which flows in strongly from the west.

The woodland becomes more extensive, with some impressive beeches, before the Way goes briefly left to a bridge of sleepers over a culvert. From here follow the track, which is the access to the Peak Rail station at Rowsley South.

A Where the railway lines begin, just before a gate, the Way veers off to the right through a squeeze stile. After briefly following the river, it strikes across meadows after a wooden stile. To the right is the high ground of Stanton Moor. On the left, by contrast, is a large engineering works.

The path continues across fields, finally reaching an occasionally muddy approach to a stile before Abbey Farm, which has extensive

■ Peak Rail is a steam railway operated by the Peak Railways Heritage Trust on the Rowsley South to Matlock Riverside section of the former Midland Railway line between Manchester Central and London St Pancras. As well as running steam trains, including a number with specific themes, Peak Rail offers exhibitions, shops and refreshments.

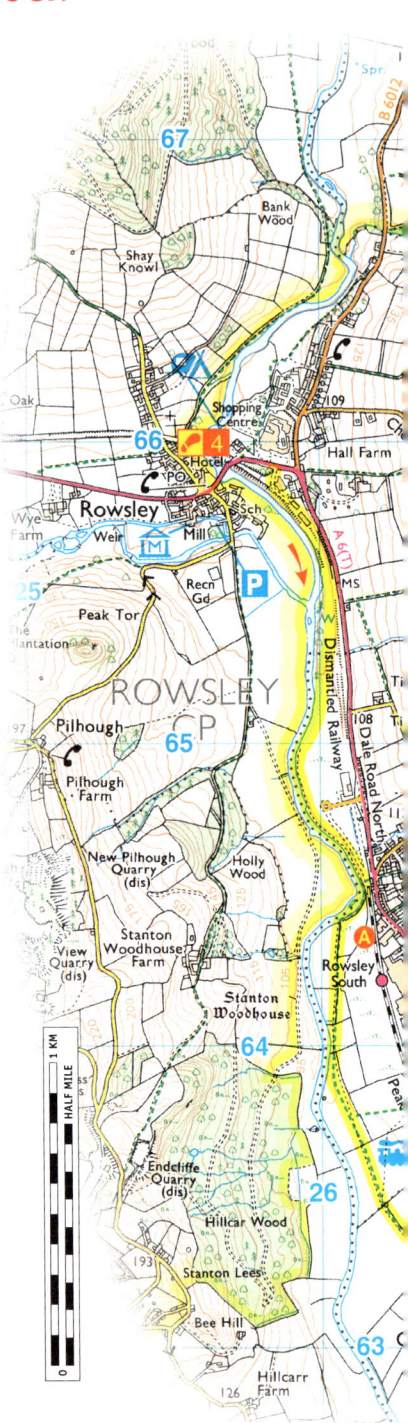

Derwent Bridge and Peak Tor, Rowsley

stables. A surfaced access road leads out past Abbey House to the quiet settlement of Churchtown, set back from the A6. At St Helen's Church, founded in about AD900, continue along Church Road.

B At the end of the churchyard, take the footpath on the right which cuts diagonally across a field behind the Stankirk boarding kennels. The two tall chimneys ahead and slightly right mark the site of the disused Mill Close Mine.

■ The prominent tower at the top of Stanton Moor's tree-clad eastern slope was built as a tribute to Earl Grey after he carried the 1832 Reform Bill through parliament. The whole of Stanton Moor is worthy of exploration, with its Nine Ladies stone circle, King Stone, Cork Stone and many Bronze Age burial mounds.

Beyond a rush-choked drainage channel the Way goes left and, on reaching the Darley Dale cricket ground by a tall, derelict scorebox, takes a track out to the B5057. Go right here on the path by the road to Darley Bridge where the Square and Compass pub has a camping and caravan site.

C Cross the bridge to the river's west bank and immediately take the gated road to Oker, spelled on the signpost here as Oaker. This road runs initially along the riverbank and you will be unlucky to be disturbed by traffic. In places, grass grows up the middle of the road, which runs along the base of a small wood then climbs slightly to the hamlet of Oker.

D In front of the second large bungalow, take the footpath which descends on the left between hedges. Soon the Way crosses meadows, touching two of the Derwent's meanders at a tangent. It then becomes a narrow, surfaced path running alongside an industrial site making asphalt roofing materials in the disused Cawdor Quarry. Considerable change is likely in the quarry area as a new relief road, superstore and housing development proceed.

The Way is soon by the river again, with extensive derelict industrial buildings to the right.

■ In St Helen's churchyard at Churchtown there is a yew tree thought to be almost 1,000 years old. It has a girth of more than 30ft (9m) and a series of stone tablets around its base commemorates outstanding actions of the Second World War – Malta, Dunkirk, River Plate, Jervis Bay, Narvik and Calais.

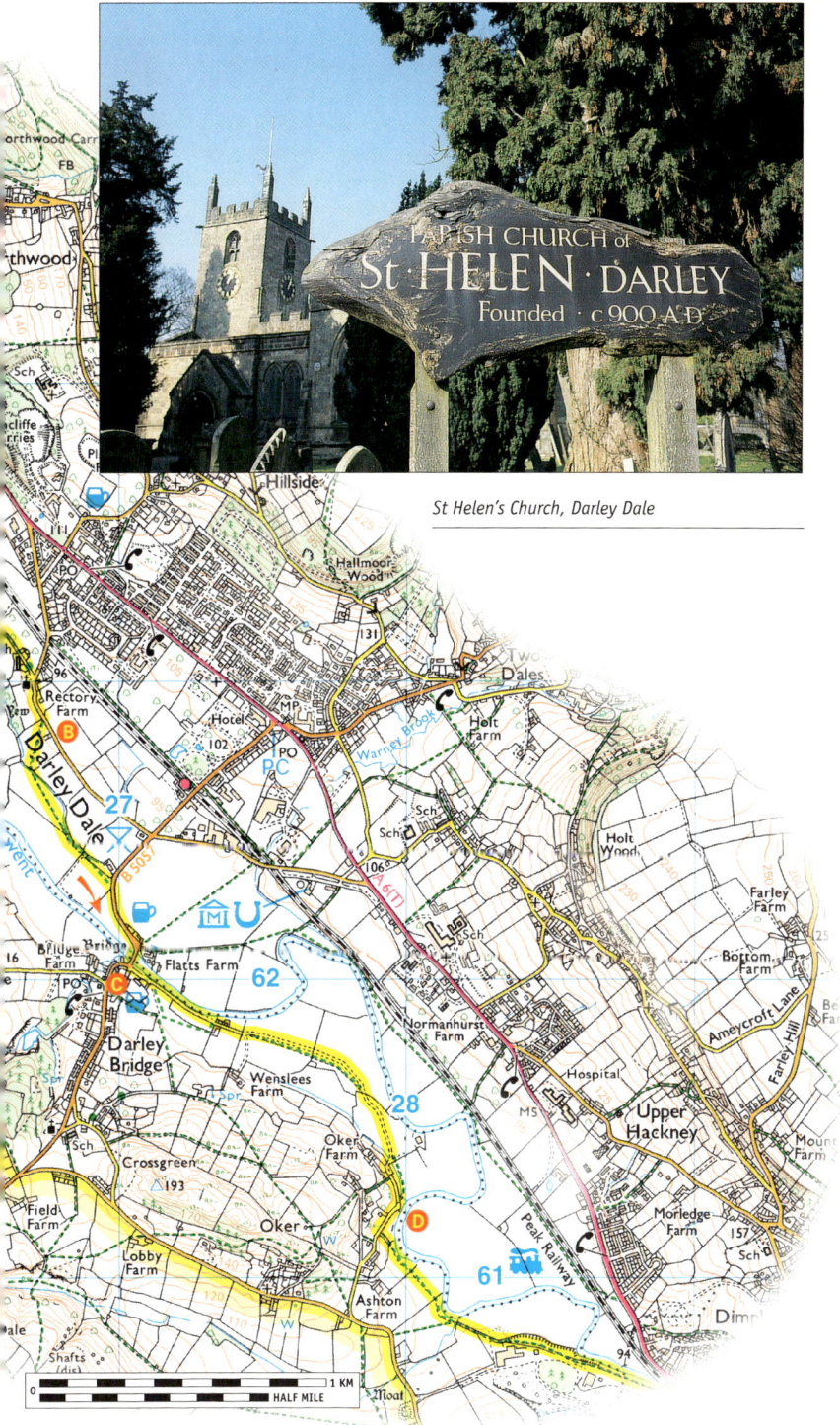

St Helen's Church, Darley Dale

■ Mill Close Mine was once one of the country's most prosperous lead mines. During the 1930s the miners were working 1,000 ft (305m) below the level of the River Derwent. Although mining ceased in 1939 because of falling lead prices and the prohibitive cost of pumping water from the mine, lead still comes from the site after being reprocessed from batteries.

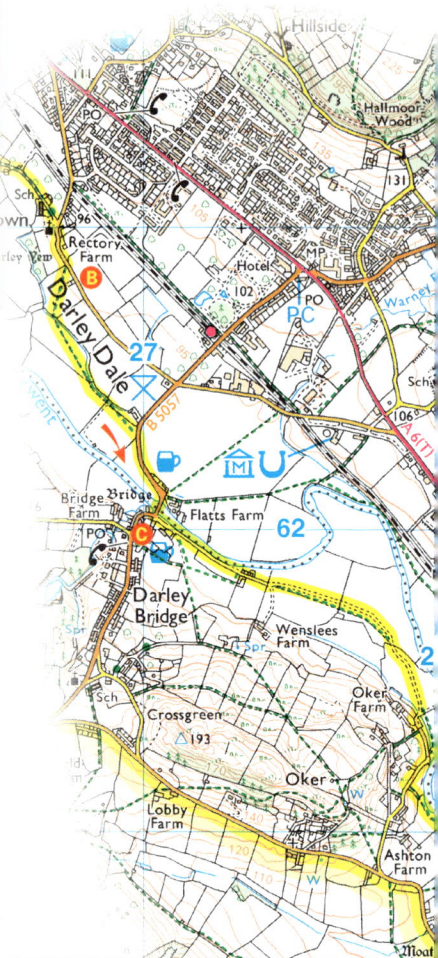

E The path passes under the bridge taken by the Peak Rail line. Despite the industrial and commercial buildings on the far bank, and the traffic noise from the busy A6 beyond them, a huge retaining wall to the right of the path creates a secluded feel and gives you the sense that you are sneaking into Matlock unnoticed. Before long you reach a car park from where both the Peak Rail and the national rail network stations are easily accessible. Turn left over Matlock Bridge for the town centre and its wide range of services. ■

Darley Bridge

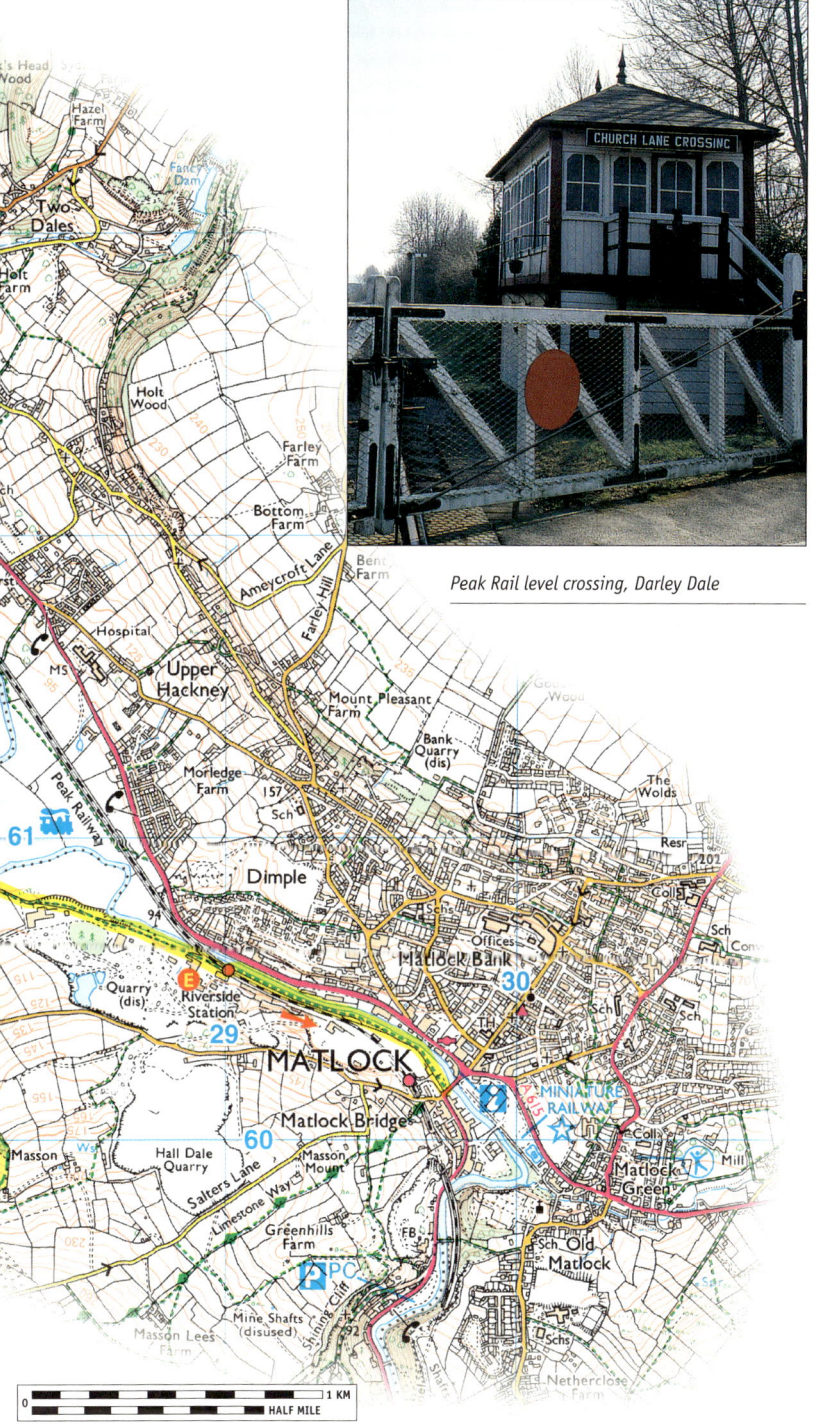

Peak Rail level crossing, Darley Dale

SECTION FIVE

Matlock to Whatstandwell

START	**Matlock**
FINISH	**Whatstandwell**
DISTANCE	**6.5 miles (10.4km)**
TERRAIN	**Two significant ascents (avoidable: see text). Paths, pavements, canal towpath**

PUBLIC TRANSPORT

To the start at Matlock, buses from Manchester, Buxton, Sheffield, Chesterfield, Nottingham and Derby; trains from Derby, Burton-on-Trent and Birmingham. From the finish at Whatstandwell, buses to Nottingham, Derby, Matlock and Manchester; trains to Matlock, Derby, Burton-on-Trent and Birmingham

FACILITIES EN ROUTE

Matlock Bath

All accommodation and refreshment facilities

Cromford

Shops, B&Bs/guesthouses

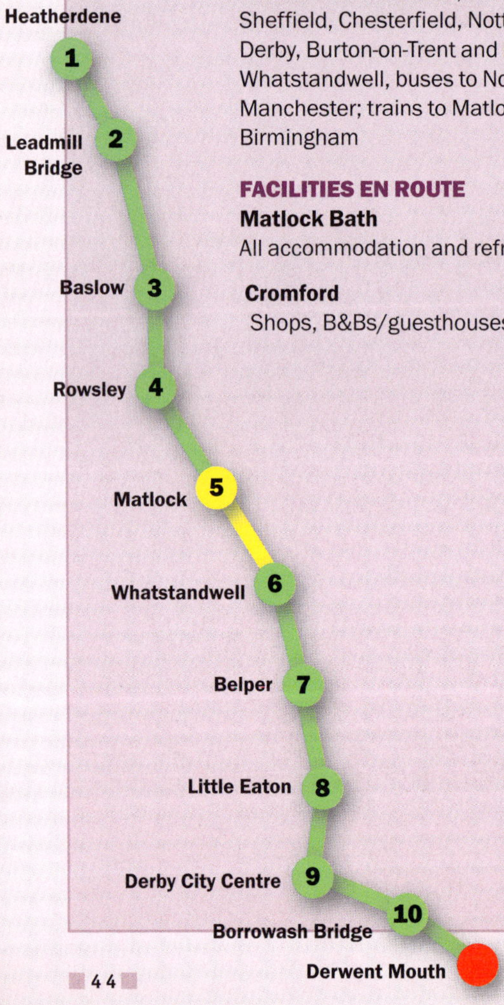

Heatherdene
1

Leadmill Bridge
2

Baslow
3

Rowsley
4

Matlock
5

Whatstandwell
6

Belper
7

Little Eaton
8

Derby City Centre
9

Borrowash Bridge
10

Derwent Mouth

DERWENT VALLEY HERITAGE WAY

Matlock Bath

This section of the Way includes two optional climbs to spectacular viewpoints, a wealth of fascinating remains from the early days of the Industrial Revolution and easy walking along a disused canal which is now a wildlife reserve.

Masson Mills Working Textiles Museum has the finest surviving and best preserved example of a Richard Arkwright cotton spinning mill as well as 100-year-old working looms, water turbines and 'Titanic' steam boilers. A little farther on, at Cromford, the street that Arkwright built for his mill-workers can be seen and there is a bookshop with a huge stock of local interest titles. At High Peak Junction the railway workshops have been faithfully restored to how they would have looked in the 1880s and a visitor centre provides information about this historic transport hub. Not far away, Leawood Pumphouse is maintained by volunteers and there are occasional steam days.

SECTION FIVE

Matlock to Whatstandwell

Note: The main route described includes a height gain of 350 ft (106m) to the top of High Tor, plus a smaller optional ascent up Pic Tor. To avoid these, simply follow the pavement alongside the A6 towards Matlock Bath.

From the east side of Matlock Bridge in the centre of the town, walk through Hall Leys Park on a broad tarmac path parallel to the river. After 200 yds (182m) notice the flood heights from 1960 and 1965 marked on the stone pillars by the footbridge.

A Beyond the park, continue into Old Matlock for 50 yds (46m), past the fronts of some fine houses. Take the footbridge on the right opposite a street lamp supported by a stone column. Beyond the bridge, bear right again on a surfaced path to come back alongside the river. Soon the limestone crags of Pic Tor, partly festooned with ivy, appear on the left.

To walk to the top of Pic Tor, follow the instructions in this paragraph. *If you wish to avoid Pic Tor, skip to the beginning of the next paragraph.* About 30 yds (27m) before you reach a railway bridge, take the path of crushed limestone which leads off to the left. With a few twists and turns, this climbs steeply to the top of Pic Tor, which is crowned by a large war memorial. There are fine views northwards over Matlock and south-east to the stark outline of Riber Castle. On the way down from Pic Tor, bear left when you get the chance and you will rejoin the route 30 yds (27m) uphill from bridge 28 AJMI. Now skip to the next but one paragraph.

Walk past the base of Pic Tor, passing under the railway bridge. When you reach a T-junction, ignore the footbridge to the right and instead go left under a stone arch marked with a cryptic cast-iron plaque 28 AJMI. From here a path of setts (paving blocks) leads uphill.

Matlock from High Tor

Follow the path upwards briefly until you see a private garage. Sharp right here, you will see an ornate entrance with a hanging sign 'To The High Tor Grounds'. These are pleasure grounds laid out in Victorian times by Frederick Charles Arkwright, after whom the path to the summit was named Arkwright's Grand Walk.

🅱 Take the obvious path uphill to the summit, passing viewpoints indicated by curved railings. *At the top of High Tor take care as you absorb the stunning views, as there is an unprotected 350 ft (106m) drop to the River Derwent.* For those with a head for heights, an excellent, airy path called Giddy Edge traverses the cliff face. *This is not recommended in wet weather, or for small children or anyone nervous of heights.*

From High Tor continue ahead, descending steeply through woodland to reach the lower station of the seasonal cable cars which go up to the Heights of Abraham. Just below the cable car station, bear half left on a path alongside the railway, then cross with care where indicated at the far end of Matlock Bath station.

The Derbyshire Wildlife Trust's Whistlestop Countryside Centre is in the station buildings. On the walk you will soon be passing Cromford

■ From High Tor the view west takes in the Heights of Abraham and the Victoria Tower. East lies Riber Castle, built by John Smedley, who transformed Matlock into a spa during the 19th century. The rich grasslands of High Tor are a stronghold of common valerian, toadflax and field scabious. The woodland on the crag below is a Site of Special Scientific Interest, noted for its large-leaved limes. Do not be surprised if rock-climbers appear over the top of the crag at High Tor. A number of challenging climbs ascend its face.

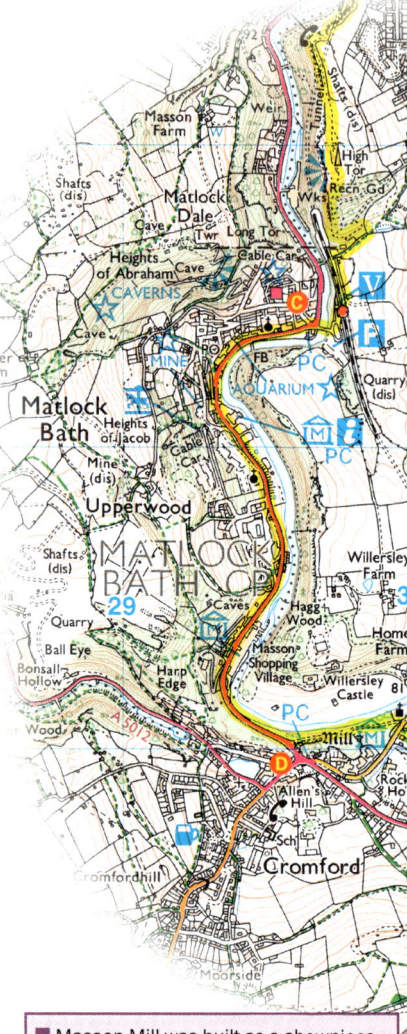

Canal, Derwentside and Wyver Lane Ponds, all Derbyshire Wildlife Trust nature reserves, so pop in and find out what you might see. From the station buildings go down through the car park to reach the A6 by the Midland pub.

C Turn left onto North Parade and follow the pavement along the west bank of the Derwent, passing many shops and cafés on the right and the 1887 Jubilee footbridge on the left. Almost opposite the footbridge is the Matlock Bath Aquarium and Petrifying Well.

Just beyond here on the left, occupying the Pavilion, is the Peak District Mining Museum and Tourist Information Centre. Soon after this, huge limestone crags rise from the east bank of the river and a tall chimney comes into view. A modest roadside sign indicates 'Derwent Valley Mills World Heritage Site'. Over the wall on your left is a leat, a curved weir and a wide area of rapids.

The chimney belongs to Masson Mills, now home to the Masson Mills Working Textiles Museum, as well as a modern shopping village and restaurant.

■ Masson Mill was built as a showpiece in 1783 by Richard Arkwright, who developed the water frame and is considered by some as the 'father of the factory system', although others dispute this. Until 1991 Masson Mills (others had been added after 1783) were the oldest mills in continuous production in the world and they remain the finest surviving, and best preserved, example of an Arkwright cotton spinning mill. The textile museum contains 100-year-old working looms, working water turbines and 'Titanic' steam boilers.

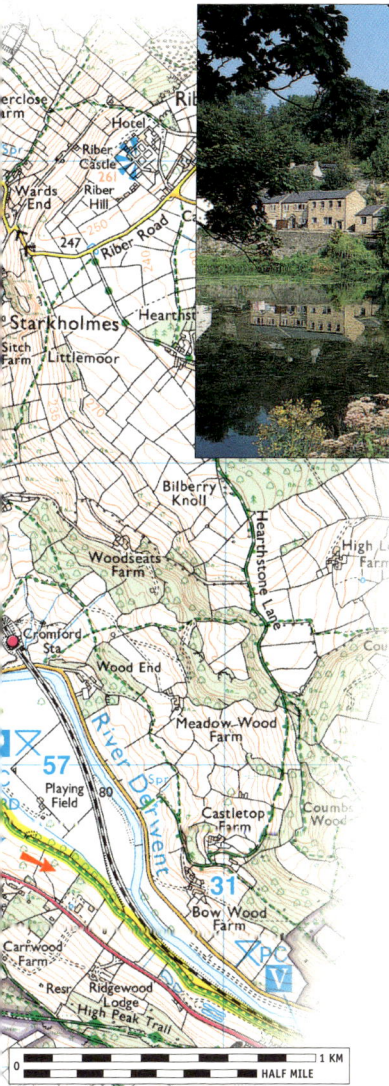

Cromford

High on the steep slope to the right of the road lies the massive half-timbered, turreted Cromford Court, redolent of another age. By the Cromford road sign, glance back to see the sheer brickwork and serried rows of windows of Masson Mills, an impressive sight rising from the river.

D Just before the traffic lights, go left between stone gateposts on Church Walk, a broad concessionary path between a limestone crag and the river. On the opposite bank lies Willersley Castle, a grand house begun in 1788. It was to be Arkwright's home but a fire broke out and Arkwright died in 1792 before the repairs were completed. It is now a hotel and conference centre run by Christian Guild Holidays. The path leads ahead to St Mary's Church, with a side path just before this, on the right, to Cromford Mill.

E Across the road from the church and the mill is Cromford Wharf, the terminus of the Cromford Canal with its typical attendant buildings. The Way follows the towpath from here

■ At Cromford, just off-route, Arkwright built North Street for his mill-workers from 1776. The village subsequently grew to service the needs of the mills and their workers. Points of interest include the village lock-up, Greyhound Pool, the ingenious 'Bear Pit', the Greyhound Hotel and, of more recent vintage, Scarthin Books, with its large stock of local interest works.

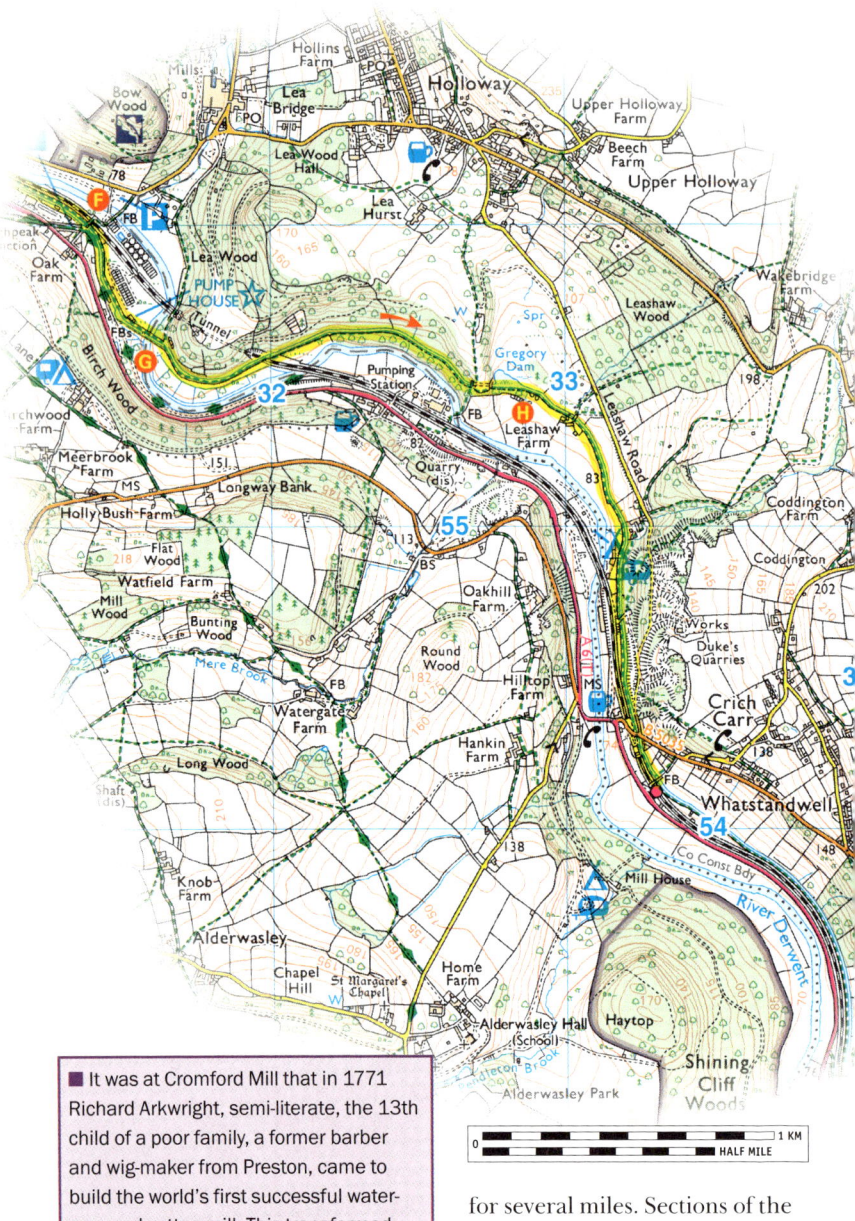

■ It was at Cromford Mill that in 1771 Richard Arkwright, semi-literate, the 13th child of a poor family, a former barber and wig-maker from Preston, came to build the world's first successful water-powered cotton mill. This transformed textile manufacturing from a cottage to a factory industry. Within 20 years Arkwright had amassed a fortune which he boasted could have liquidated the entire national debt. The whole complex, which includes tours of the mill, information, refreshments and a bookshop, is being carefully restored.

for several miles. Sections of the canal are shallow, reedy and tree-lined, occasionally used by canoeists and frequently by little grebes.

After a mile the canal reaches High Peak Junction. Here, where there are picnic tables, a shop, toilets and an information centre, the Way crosses to the west side of the canal.

■ The surviving railway workshops at High Peak Junction are among the world's oldest. Built around 1830, they have been faithfully restored to how they would have looked in the 1880s. At the Wharf Shed, 275 yds (250m) south, cargo was transferred from the Cromford Canal to the Cromford and High Peak Railway, built between 1825 and 1830, for the hilly crossing of the Peak District. A visitor centre provides a wealth of information about this historic transport hub. The railway has now been converted to the High Peak Trail, a very popular walking and cycling route.

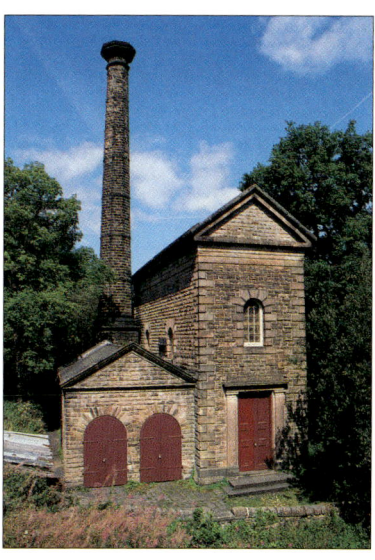

Leawood Pumphouse

F From High Peak Junction you are following the line of the old railway alongside the canal. Almost immediately you reach the Wharf Shed. Continue for 100 yds (91m) then go left at a fingerpost to regain the canal bank opposite Leawood Pumphouse, with its towering brick chimney.

G Immediately after the pumphouse, the canal narrows as it becomes an aqueduct above the river. From here it winds alongside the Derbyshire Wildlife Trust's Derwentside Nature Reserve. After a short way the canal crosses the railway on an aqueduct. The railway in turn disappears into a tunnel 20 yds (18m) to the left. Below, on the right, is the river and, beyond that, the A6. It's intriguing to see all these modes of transport threading their way down the valley. Soon you reach Gregory Tunnel, where the towpath is guarded by a handrail.

If you are walking the stretch of canal between the aqueduct and Gregory Tunnel in spring, keep a lookout for the locally well-known drifts of wild daffodils. Watch also for water voles, a threatened species that

is the subject of a DWT project to protect remaining habitats and populations.

H Beyond the tunnel, the river comes close to the canal again. Soon there's an idyllic house on the opposite bank at Robin Hood, a hamlet not named on the 1:25,000 map.

■ Leawood Pumphouse contains a steam-powered beam engine which raises water from the River Derwent to the Cromford Canal. The main beam is 33 ft (10m) long and weighs 27 tonnes. The pumphouse is maintained by volunteers and there are occasional steaming days.

The Way passes coppiced woodland on the opposite bank to reach a road. About 60 yds (55m) down to the right is the Derwent Hotel; to the left the road leads to Crich and its famous Tramway Museum. Continue alongside the canal for 100 yds (91m) beyond the road to a footbridge on the right that leads to Whatstandwell station. ■

SECTION SIX

Whatstandwell to Belper

START	**Whatstandwell station**
FINISH	**Belper Market Place**
DISTANCE	**5.6 miles (9.1km)**
TERRAIN	**Canal towpath, woodland and field paths, minor roads**

PUBLIC TRANSPORT

To the start at Whatstandwell, and from the finish at Belper, buses link to Nottingham, Derby, Matlock and Manchester; trains link to Matlock, Derby, Burton-on-Trent and Birmingham

FACILITIES EN ROUTE

Whatstandwell

Pub, restaurant, B&Bs/guesthouses, shop. Nearest youth hostel – Shining Cliff

Ambergate

Pub, restaurant, café/tearooms, shops, public toilets, children's play area, PO. Nearest youth hostel – Shining Cliff, Ambergate, Nearest campsites – Firs Farm Caravan and Camping Park, Ambergate, Birchwood Farm Caravan Park

Broadholm

Pub, children's play area. Nearest youth hostel – Shining Cliff, Ambergate, Nearest campsite – Broadholm Lane Farm Nursery

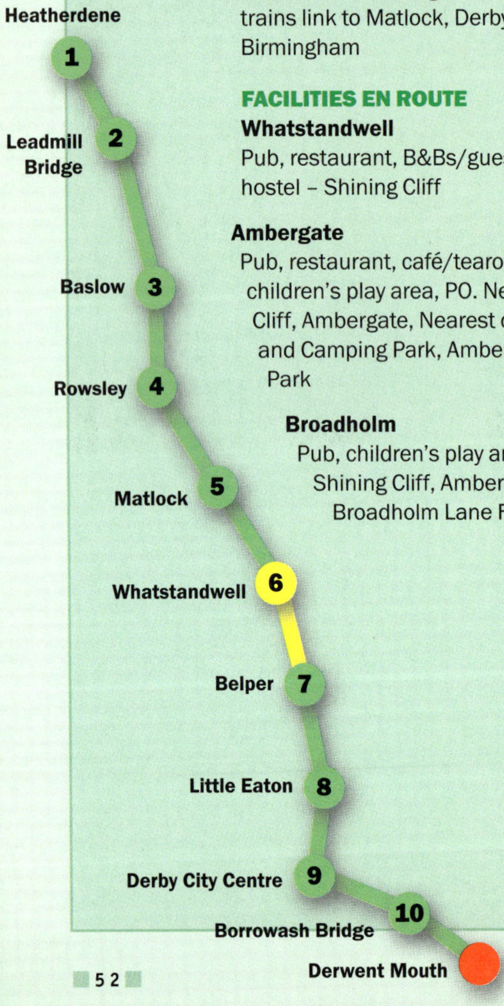

Heatherdene **1**

Leadmill Bridge **2**

Baslow **3**

Rowsley **4**

Matlock **5**

Whatstandwell **6**

Belper **7**

Little Eaton **8**

Derby City Centre **9**

Borrowash Bridge **10**

Derwent Mouth

DERWENT VALLEY HERITAGE WAY

The Cromford Canal, a local nature reserve near Ambergate

After initially following a disused canal, now a Site of Special Scientific Interest (SSSI) and local nature reserve, the Way then takes to woods and fields beyond Ambergate before passing a large pond as it heads for Belper, a town retaining much of its intriguing industrial past.

At Shining Cliff Woods there are the remains of a huge yew tree said to be 2,000 years old and, according to legend, the origin of the nursery rhyme *Rock-a-hye-baby*. Near Belper Bridge the original North Mill, one of the town's various mills, now houses the Dorwent Valley Visitor Centre and interpretative museum.

SECTION SIX

Whatstandwell to Belper

From Whatstandwell station take the footbridge over the track to the canal towpath. Turn right along a stretch where canal, rail, road and river are all close. Wildlife interest is provided by moorhens and mallards on the canal, and jays in the adjacent trees of Crich Chase.

To the west lies the huge expanse of Shining Cliff Woods. The canal continues south and, just before it reaches Ambergate, it veers away from the road and railway. At an ivy-covered bridge beyond the redbrick Chase Farm, leave the canal, taking a step-stile by a gate onto Chase Road.

A Turn downhill and you soon pass under a railway bridge and reach the A6.

Go left here on the pavement by the road, and watch for the River Amber

The Cromford Canal

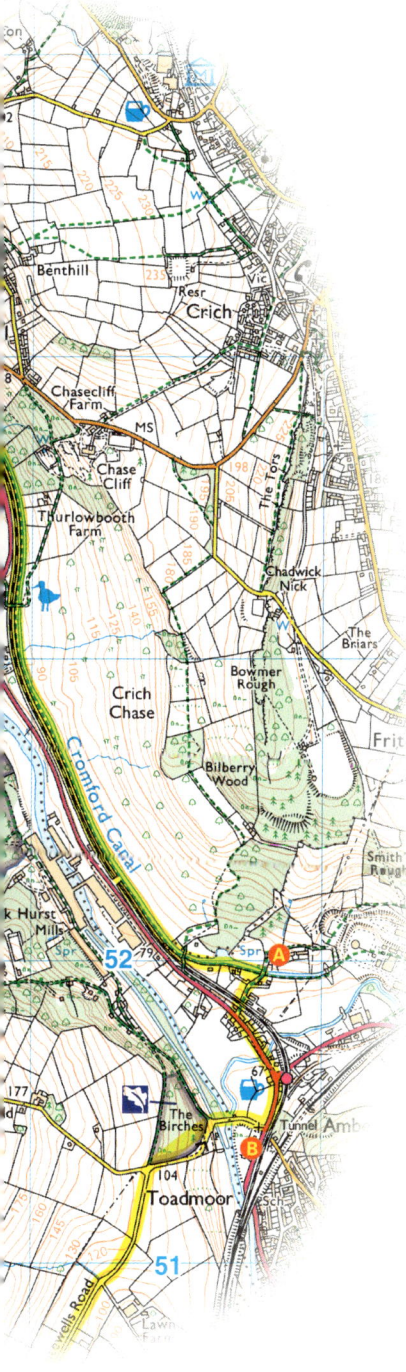

■ Betty Kenny (Kate Kenyon) and her husband Luke lived during the late 18th century in a huge yew tree reputed to be 2,000 years old, the remains of which are still visible in Shining Cliff Woods. The Kenyons raised eight children and legend suggests that a bough they hollowed out as a cradle was the origin of the nursery rhyme *Rock-a-bye-baby*. Luke was a charcoal burner and he and Betty became favourites of the Hurt family who had their portraits painted by James Ward of the Royal Academy.

under the road. This is the safest place to cross the A6. Continue past the Hurt Arms Hotel.

≋ 🚌 P Ambergate station is close by. Take the road opposite the Hurt Arms, under the bridge, then follow the signpost to the station on the right. A little way up this road, steps lead up and round to the station.

B Follow the road beyond the Hurt Arms then, immediately after the cricket ground, turn right by the church into Holly Lane. Soon you reach Halfpenny Bridge, an old toll bridge over the Derwent. Look right to see the confluence of the Amber and Derwent Rivers.

■ The Whatstandwell to Ambergate section of the Cromford Canal, not used by commercial boats since 1944, is now a SSSI and a Local Nature Reserve, owned by Derbyshire County Council and managed by Derbyshire Wildlife Trust with help from DCC and English Nature. Plant life includes bankside species such as water mint and meadowsweet. Dragonflies and damselflies are a frequent sight and the canal is one of the remaining strongholds in Derbyshire for the water vole.

Immediately beyond the bridge, bear right on a track indicating the Betty Kenny Trail and YHA. After 30 yds (27m) go left on a concessionary path signposted to Whitewells Road. Pass through this area, called The Birches and owned by the Woodland Trust. Take the path parallel to the road as it rises through the wood and when it emerges, follow the single-track road called Whitewells Lane, directly opposite. Pass the access drives to Lawn Farm and Dairywood Farm. A wood lies beyond this, with a stile on the left immediately after it.

C Go down the field, parallel to the edge of the wood, continuing ahead through a squeeze stile and bearing slightly right, as indicated by the waymark, heading for the walled extension of Yewtree Wood to the right. Follow the wall of the wood round to the right where you will reach the access track to Lawn Cottage, which is off to the left. Ignore the cottage and continue ahead on this track.

It passes the reed-fringed Wyver

Lane Pool, a nature reserve owned by the Derbyshire Wildlife Trust. A hide by the road provides a handy viewpoint over the pool. In summer it's a magnet for swallows and swifts, damselflies and dragonflies, and the occasional hobby, the most dashing of hawks. The track becomes slightly more formal as Wyver Lane soon arrives in Belper at a line of old millworkers' cottages with riverside gardens.

D On reaching the main road, bear left on the pavement, and immediately before Belper Bridge, keep your eyes open for Calder's Corner on the left, a tiny patch of grass with an information board and a fine view across the Derwent to the North and East Mills. Continue across the bridge, from where the Horseshoe Weir is well seen as a foaming curve, with the River Gardens beyond. A diversion across the North Mill car park to the path over the sluices gives access to these delightful gardens, a Strutt family gift of 1905.

Weir and mills from Belper Bridge

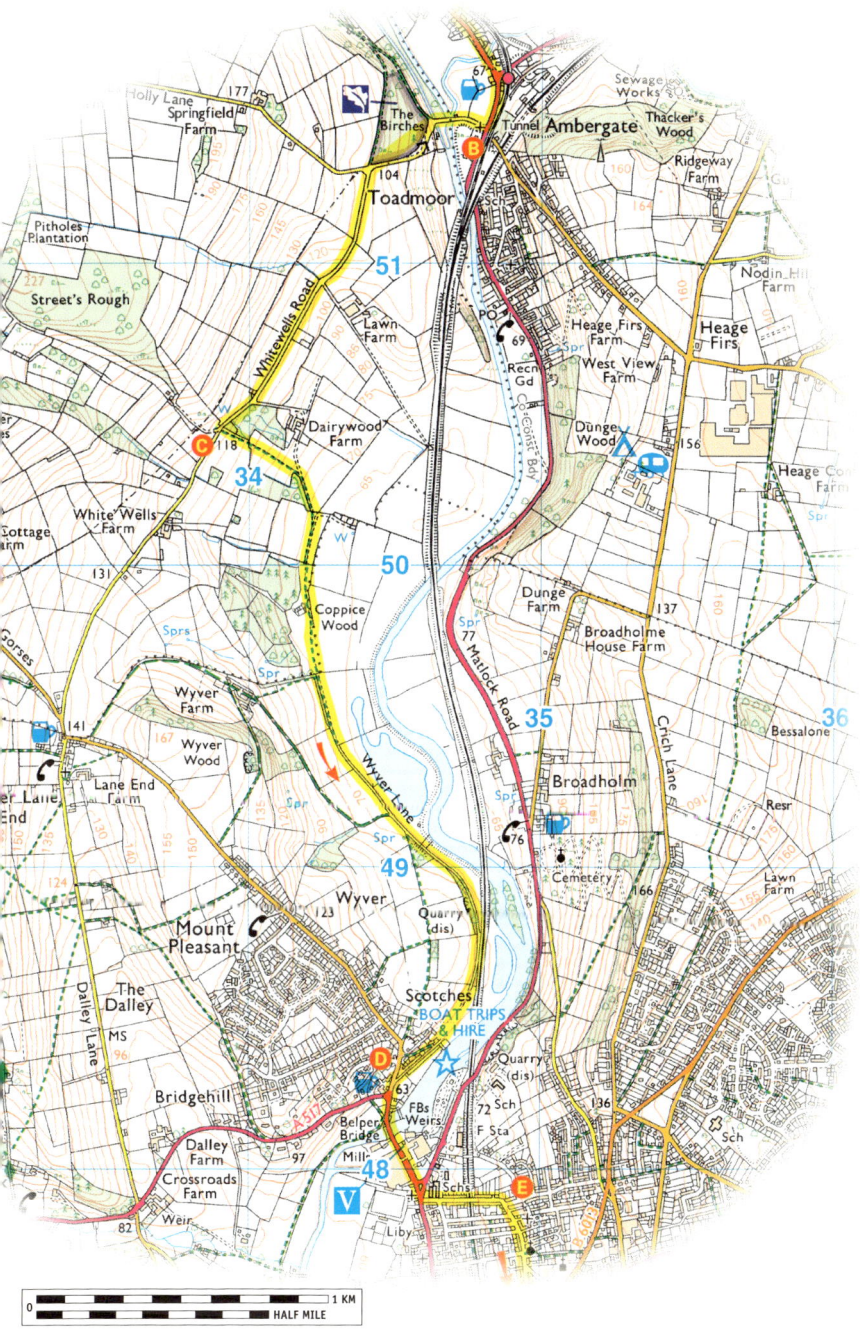

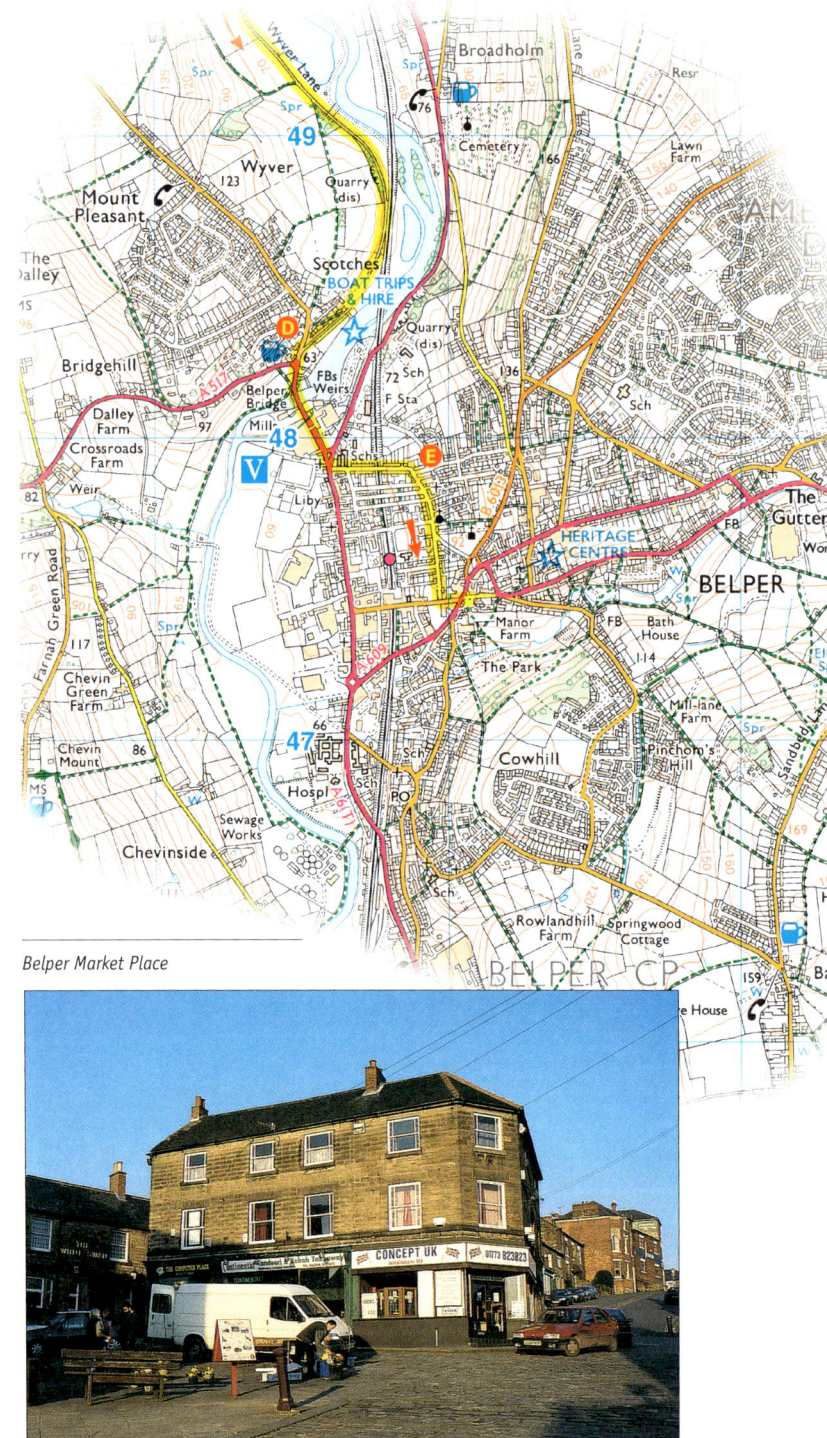

Belper Market Place

Millworkers' houses, Long Row, Belper

Pass the Mills, going under an arch and then cross to The Triangle, where there is another information board. Cross the A6, head in the Derby direction for 30 yds (27m) then go left into Long Row. This street is a wonderful piece of living history, cobbled and lined by millworkers' cottages.

E At the top of Long Row turn right into Green Lane. As you pass George and Joseph Streets look out for 'The Clusters', blocks of four houses built for the mill supervisors. Beyond the Unitarian Sunday School, marked with a carved stone dated 1721 – 1855, you will reach King Street opposite the War Memorial Gardens. Turn right, downhill, for the town centre and railway station or left, uphill, for the Market Place. Originally this was known as The Green, before being upgraded to become the Market Place in the 1830s. Paved in 1881, it was once surrounded by nine pubs. Recent renovation has included the provision of an information board by the Belper Historical Society. Close by is the Heritage Centre, based in St. John's Chapel. ■

■ Belper's industrial history is closely tied to the Strutt family. North Mill was built in 1804 for cotton yarn manufacture by William Strutt, who refined the concept of 'fireproof' iron-framed buildings. Ownership of Belper's various mills eventually passed from the Strutt family to the English Sewing Cotton Company, which had the enormous brick-built East Mill constructed in 1912. The original North Mill now houses the Derwent Valley Visitor Centre and interpretative museum.

7 SECTION SEVEN

Belper to Little Eaton

START	**Belper Market Place**
FINISH	**Little Eaton**
DISTANCE	**4.8 miles (7.7km)**
TERRAIN	**Footpaths, tracks, pavement by road**

PUBLIC TRANSPORT
To the start at Belper, buses from Nottingham, Derby, Matlock and Manchester; trains from Matlock, Derby, Burton-on-Trent and Birmingham. From the finish at Little Eaton, buses to Belper, Derby, Mansfield and Heanor

FACILITIES EN ROUTE
Milford
Pub, restaurant, B&Bs/guesthouses, shops, children's play area, Nearest youth hostel – Shining Cliff, Ambergate, nearest campsite – Broadholm Lane Farm Nursery

Makeney
Pub, restaurant, hotels, shops, children's play area. Nearest youth hostel – Shining Cliff, Ambergate, nearest campsite – Broadholm Lane Farm Nursery

Duffield
Pub, restaurant, café/tearooms, B&Bs/guesthouses, banks, shops, public toilets, children's play area, PO. Nearest youth hostel – Shining Cliff, Ambergate, nearest campsite – Broadholm Lane Farm Nursery, railway station.

Little Eaton
Pub, restaurant, café/tearooms, shops, children's play area, PO. Nearest youth hostel – Shining Cliff, Ambergate, nearest campsite – Broadholm Lane Farm Nursery

Heatherdene — 1
Leadmill Bridge — 2
Baslow — 3
Rowsley — 4
Matlock — 5
Whatstandwell — 6
Belper — 7
Little Eaton — 8
Derby City Centre — 9
Borrowash Bridge — 10
Derwent Mouth

Weirs at Milford

The Way negotiates the undulating eastern side of the Derwent Valley and, as it does, passes patchwork fields, tall chimneys hinting of past industry and an ancient bridge over a disused quarry, all the while not far from signs of urban life.

Belper Park is a remnant of an old Royal forest. In the Middle Ages it was owned by the Duchy of Lancaster and used for breeding deer. Peckwash Mill, built in 1805, became one of the biggest paper mills in the country. Its spectacular chimney was added in 1895 but the emission of smoke upset a neighbour, a consequence that led to the demise of the business. Stone from the nearby Rigga Quarry area was used in the construction of Derby Cathedral and other notable buildings around the Midlands.

Mill chimney at Milford

From the Market Place, go through The Coppice car park and take the path downhill from there across Belper Park to Coppice Brook.

A few yards beyond the footbridge, take the right fork in the path then after another 15 yds (14m), turn right at a DVHW signpost. This path soon reaches a remarkably sloping football pitch. Go uphill, to the left of the posts and follow the waymarks, continuing to gain height, to reach more housing. Soon you come to the junction of Bargate Road and Holbrook Road.

A Turn right, downhill, along Holbrook Road for 120 yds (110m), then go left on Wildersley Road, a track which visibly dips then rises ahead, arrow-straight. As the Way rises the view to the right is across a patchwork of fields and woods on the sides of the Derwent Valley.

By the stone buildings at Wildersley Farm, go right, via a stile, to skirt the left-hand edge of a wood. The Way contours across the valley side, with a view down to Milford. An impressive chimney is prominent in the centre of the village while, across the valley, the apparent tower is an air shaft for the railway tunnelling beneath.

B Cross Shaw Lane, passing above Milford. *Take care here as the barbed wire fence on the right is very close to the path.* Continue through a series of squeeze stiles, crossing a couple of fields to reach a tiny paddock. From here, bear right down Dark Lane into the quiet backwater of Makeney passing, or possibly visiting, the Holly Bush Inn, an absolute gem of a rural pub. Grade II listed, it dates from the late 17th century and Dick Turpin is known to have been a customer.

C At the bottom of Holly Bush Lane go left, taking the pavement by the road. This climbs slightly, giving

> ■ Milford, which lies a short way off the route, is wedged alongside a curve of the Derwent where the high land on either side constricts the valley. The cottages, churches and pubs, built alongside the cotton and bleach works as part of Strutt's industrial community, can still be seen.

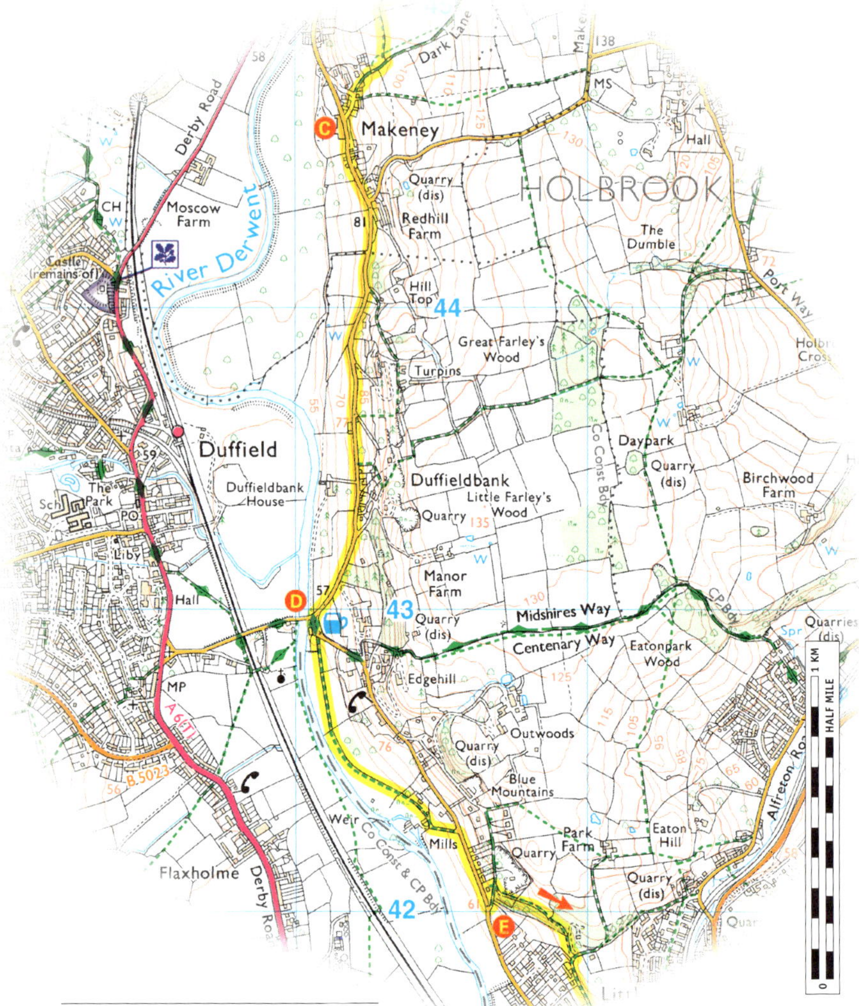

Sign by the Bridge Inn, Duffield Bridge

The Holly Bush Inn, Makeney

a view across the flat meadows by the Derwent. Pass Red Lane and continue ahead. Away to the right, Duffield village is visible across the Derwent's floodplain, with the river's meandering course marked by lines of trees. To the left are woods with occasional houses half-hidden on the slopes. Follow the pavement downhill to the Derwent at Duffield Bridge and the adjacent Bridge Inn, which has tables overlooking the river.

D Pass the front of the Bridge Inn and take the path ahead through grassy fields. Before long this becomes a narrow passage between tall stone walls. A huge brick chimney stands to the left of the path, with the buildings of Peckwash Mill to the right. The path follows the railings of the mill's access drive up to the road.

Turn right and take the pavement for 250 yds (228m) then turn sharp left up an old paved path. This is Rigga Lane. Go uphill, ignoring the

> ■ Built by Thomas Tempest in 1805, Peckwash Mill became one of the biggest paper mills in the country. The magnificent brick chimney was added in 1895 but in 1906 a neighbour was awarded a permanent injunction restraining Tempest and Son from emitting smoke from the chimney. This caused the demise of the business shortly afterwards. The mill is now a private residence.

Packhorse bridge over Rigga Quarry, Little Eaton

first path on the right but taking the second, where a waymark on a wooden rail shows the way.

E This soon crosses a narrow stone bridge which spans the disused Rigga Quarry. This has been reclaimed by trees since its heyday. Narrow and tall squeeze stiles on the path beyond the quarry may mean rucksacks have to be removed to negotiate them. *Pushchairs would be impossible here*.

On reaching Vicarage Lane, go right, downhill, for about 150 yds (137m) until you reach a point where a couple of tarmac lanes join from the left by a mysterious sign announcing 'SEA WIFE'.

F At this point bear slightly left on the lane past the top of the churchyard and then follow the footpath on the right as the tarmac surface veers left. This brings you down into Little Eaton opposite a pharmacy. Go straight ahead, crossing a disused railway and the Bottle Brook to reach Alfreton Road. ■

■ Gritstone from Rigga Lane Quarry was used for whetstones (for sharpening scythes), kerbs, sinks and troughs. Stone from this immediate area was used in the construction of Derby Cathedral, Birmingham Town Hall and Trent Bridge at Nottingham. The footbridge spanning the workings was most probably used by the quarrymen on their way to work.

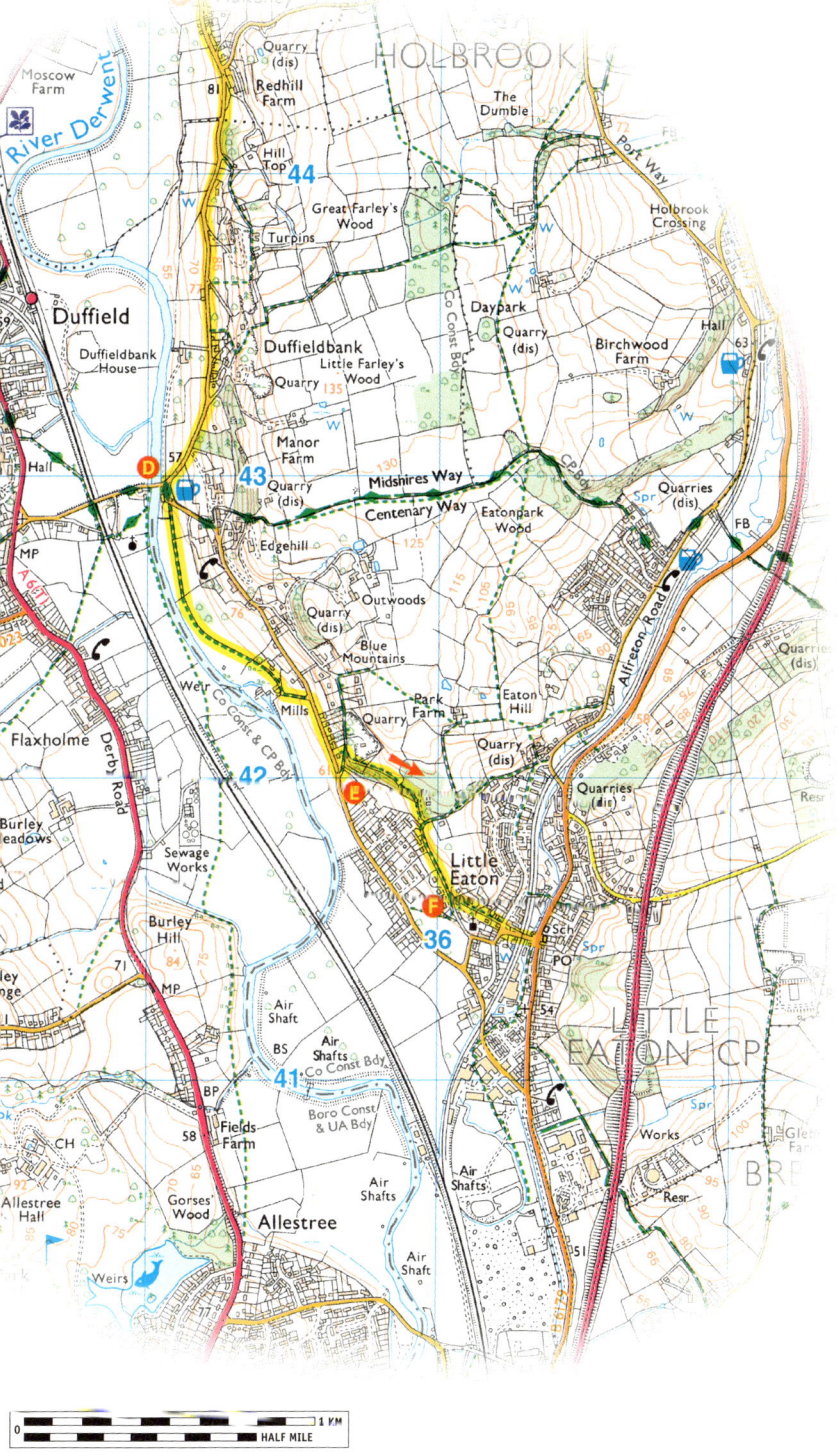

SECTION EIGHT

Little Eaton to Derby

START	**Little Eaton**
FINISH	**Derby City Centre**
DISTANCE	**4.5 miles (7.2km)/5.1 miles (8.2km)**
TERRAIN	**Cycleway, river meadows, parkland, riverside path**

PUBLIC TRANSPORT

To the start at Little Eaton, buses from Belper, Derby, Mansfield and Heanor. From the finish at Derby, extensive bus and train connections

FACILITIES EN ROUTE

Allestree

Pub, restaurant, café/tearooms, banks, shops, children's play area, PO. Nearest youth hostel – Shining Cliff, Ambergate, nearest campsite – Broadholm Lane Farm Nursery

Derby

Pubs, restaurants, tearooms, hotels, B&Bs/guesthouses, shops, PO, banks, leisure centres. Nearest campsite – Beechwood Park, Elvaston

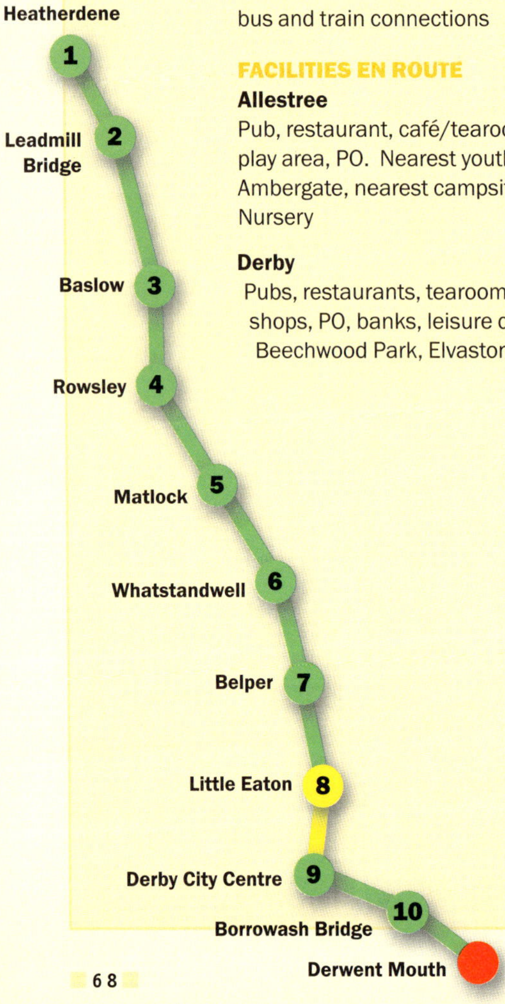

Heatherdene
1

Leadmill
Bridge
2

Baslow **3**

Rowsley **4**

5
Matlock

6
Whatstandwell

Belper **7**

Little Eaton **8**

Derby City Centre **9**

10
Borrowash Bridge

Derwent Mouth

Derby Cathedral

Initially following a cycleway, the Way then crosses river meadows to Darley Abbey, once a village and now a quiet suburb with a fascinating industrial heritage. It then approaches Derby city centre via Darley Abbey Park, a riverside path and museum.

The park features an informative tree trail which links 30 different species. It also houses national collections of viburnum and hydrangeas. Farther on, Derby Industrial Museum (free entry) focuses on local industries. including railways and Rolls-Royce aero engines. Formerly a silk mill, in the 18th century it employed 300 people, enabling it to claim to be, in effect, the world's first modern factory. Nearby is a picturesque pub which dates from 1530.

From the junction with the road called The Town, go south past the Queen's Head Inn and the smithy to reach a cycle route parallel to Alfreton Road. Follow this until you approach a large roundabout.

A On reaching the roundabout, turn right into Ford Lane. Continue as far as the railway and take the footpath on the left immediately before it. Climb the steps, turn right to take the footway alongside the A38 over the railway, then descend the steps on the right. At the base of the steps turn left, then left again to pass under the road.

B Just beyond the underpass a fingerpost points the way across flood meadows. New wooden posts carrying waymarks show the line of the route, just to the left of an obvious track.

Three unkempt, fenced mounds marking air shafts about 300 yds (274m) apart stand above the meadows, which are used for turf production with strips skimmed from the flat surface. The Way passes just to the right of the first mound then just left of the second and third.

■ The Queen's Head Inn, built in 1835, was originally called the Delvers' Inn after the local 'delvers' who worked in the quarries. The Gangway, a form of railroad which linked with the Derby Canal to the south, once ran behind the pub, connecting to the collieries at Kilburn and Denby, a few miles to the north. The nearby blacksmith's shop would have been kept busy shoeing the horses that worked this route.

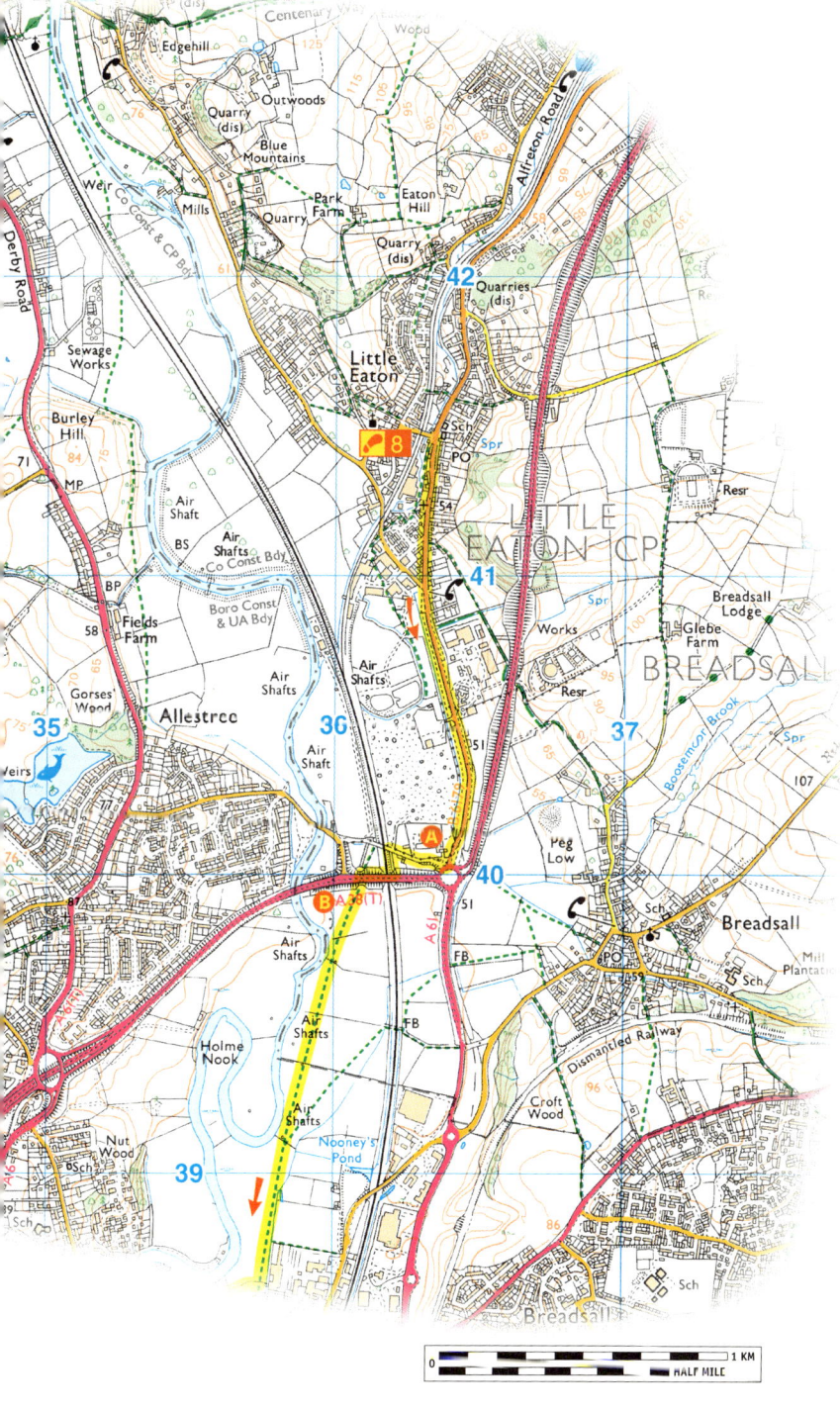

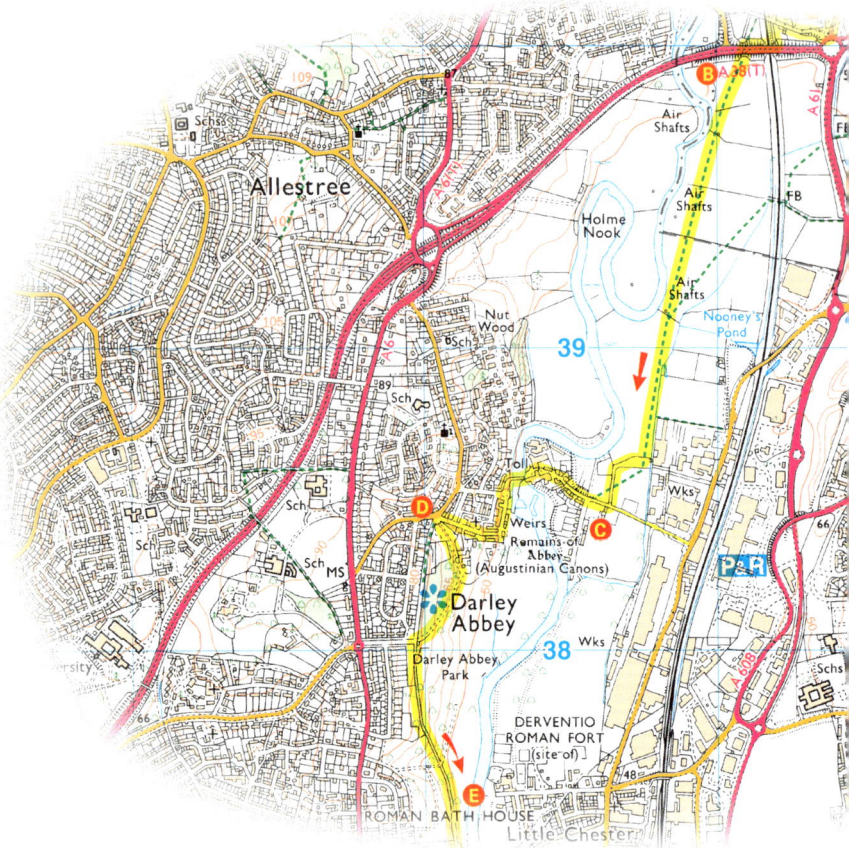

Passing to the left of a moat-like fishing lake with trees on its island, the route comes alongside a wooden fence with an industrial area to the left. Continue ahead across sometimes damp ground, then bear right along the hedge at the end of the field to a new gate. Follow the track ahead to emerge opposite Derby Rugby Club.

C Turn right along Haslam's Lane into Darley Abbey Mills, passing among the buildings on a private road to reach a toll bridge. (A toll is payable but may not always be collected). Beyond the bridge is Darley Abbey village, now a northern suburb of Derby. From the bridge turn left by a wide stretch of the River Derwent to reach a fine weir. A small public garden with benches looks over the weir and across to the mill.

Go ahead past The Square and the Darley Abbey Inn, a superb building of warm stone, then turn right to climb New Road. This allows a closer look at some of the attractive remains of this old industrial hamlet, including the Old Darley Abbey School built in 1826. This two-storey redbrick building with a clock in the centre has houses for the master and mistress at either end.

Notice in Darley Abbey village

D At the top of New Road turn sharp left into Darley Abbey Park, following a path between rhododendrons to reach a café and toilets. From the attractive terrace there are good views across the park.

Follow the upper path through the park, with a spacious view down on the left to the Derwent. At the park gates go left by the lodge to discover, as you follow a path by a stone-edged grassy area, that you are still actually in the park.

E The path gradually loses height.

The Darley Abbey Inn

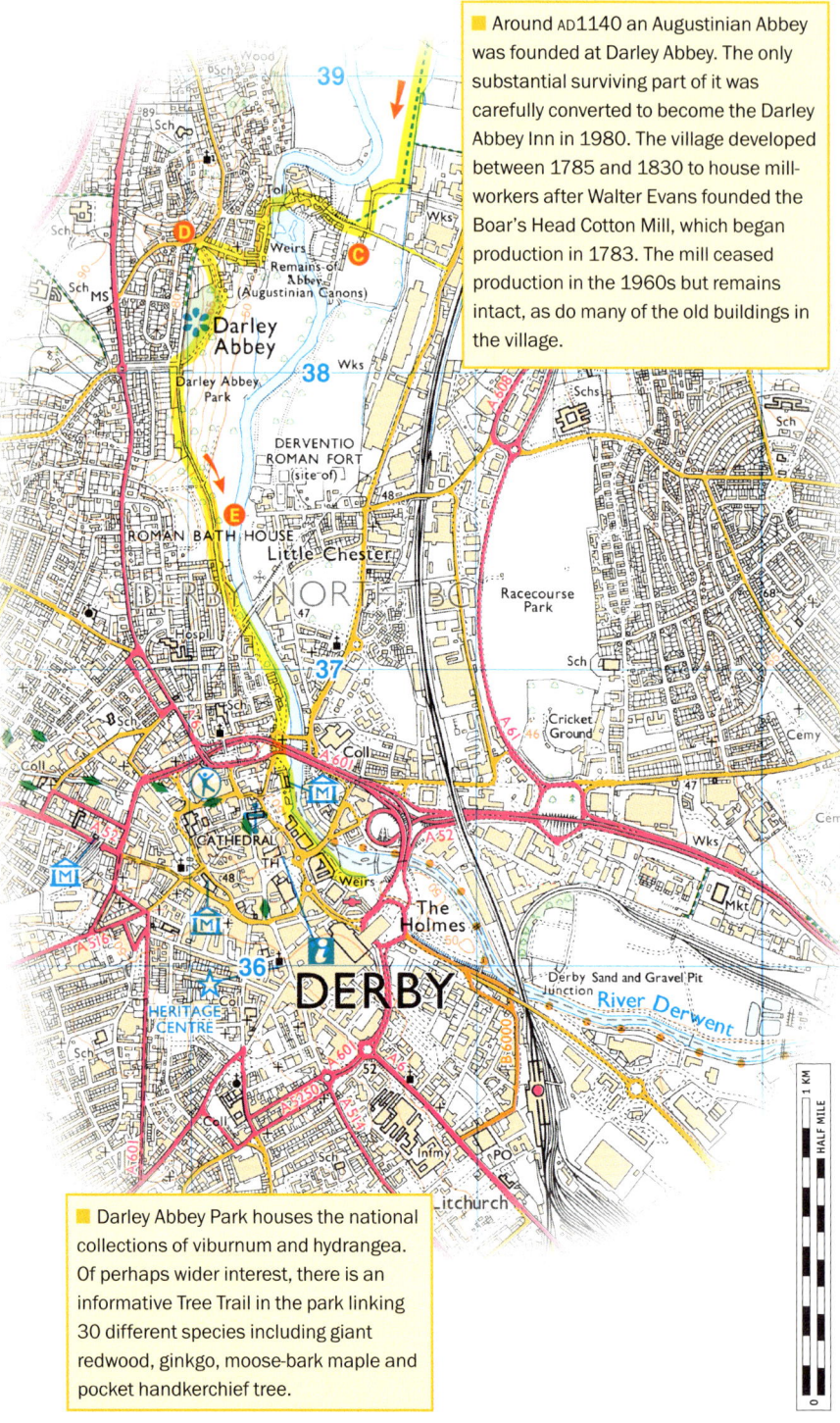

■ Around AD1140 an Augustinian Abbey was founded at Darley Abbey. The only substantial surviving part of it was carefully converted to become the Darley Abbey Inn in 1980. The village developed between 1785 and 1830 to house mill-workers after Walter Evans founded the Boar's Head Cotton Mill, which began production in 1783. The mill ceased production in the 1960s but remains intact, as do many of the old buildings in the village.

■ Darley Abbey Park houses the national collections of viburnum and hydrangea. Of perhaps wider interest, there is an informative Tree Trail in the park linking 30 different species including giant redwood, ginkgo, moose-bark maple and pocket handkerchief tree.

Darley Abbey Park, near the edge of Derby

and comes nearer to the river. At a set of metal bollards go left across the grass to another, lower set of metal bollards on a path at the edge of the park. On the opposite bank of the Derwent is the site of the Roman fort of Derventio, its outlines now hidden beneath football pitches.

Continue past the Derwent Rowing Club, following the riverside path into a more built-up area. Pass under a bridge carrying Derby's inner ring road soon to reach Derby Industrial Museum, which has free entry and is well worth a visit. This also marks the southern boundary of the Derwent Valley Mills World Heritage Site. Close by, on Queen Street, is the picturesque Old Dolphin pub which dates from 1530.

Continue from the museum along the river. Cross Derwent Street with care to an area where the river widens. A sizeable population of Canada geese and ducks occupies the river in front of the steps on the curving south bank. Just 100 yds (91m) behind the river steps is Derby bus station.

≈ 🚌 🅿 For Derby railway station, continue along the riverside path for another 500 yds (455m) then, by an obvious signpost immediately before the railway bridge across the river, turn right along Railway Terrace. ■

> ■ Derby Industrial Museum stands on the site of John Lombe's silk mill where, at the beginning of the 18th century, 300 people were employed making silk thread. This was the first time such a large number of workers had been together on one site making this, in effect, the world's first modern factory. Now, as a museum, the old mill focuses on Derbyshire industries, including railway research and Rolls-Royce aero engines.

SECTION NINE

Derby City Centre to Borrowash Bridge

START   **Derby City Centre**
FINISH   **Borrowash Bridge/Borrowash centre**
DISTANCE   **4.9 miles (7.9km)/5.3 miles (8.5km)**
TERRAIN   **Level walking on well-surfaced riverside paths**

PUBLIC TRANSPORT

Extensive bus and train connections to the start at Derby. From the finish at Borrowash, buses to Derby and Nottingham

FACILITIES EN ROUTE

Derby
Pubs, restaurants, tearooms, hotels, B&Bs/guesthouses, shops, PO, banks, leisure centres. Nearest campsite – Beechwood Park, Elvaston

Borrowash
Pubs, restaurant, shops, PO, banks. Nearest campsite – Beechwood Park, Elvaston

Heatherdene — 1
Leadmill Bridge — 2
Baslow — 3
Rowsley — 4
Matlock — 5
Whatstandwell — 6
Belper — 7
Little Eaton — 8
Derby City Centre — 9
Borrowash Bridge — 10
Derwent Mouth

DERWENT VALLEY HERITAGE WAY

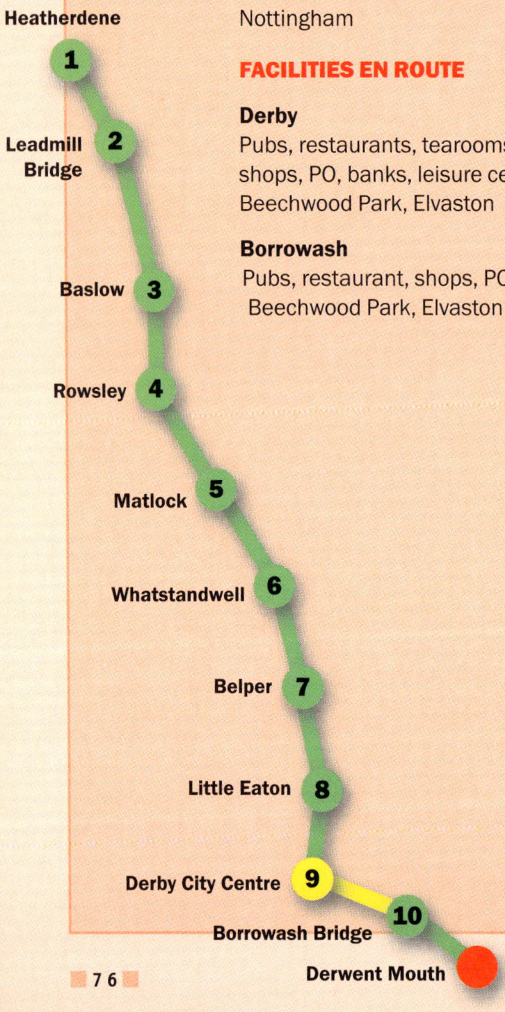

The Derwent flowing quietly near Alvaston

For much of this section the Way closely follows the south bank of the river. The landscape includes weirs and lagoons, meadows and woodland, as well as modern developments, including a futuristic football stadium.

The Pride Park area, the original site of Derby's railway manufacturing industry, once employed 6,000 people but by the early 1990s was derelict. A £37 million regeneration programme has encouraged a commercial revival with new industrial units rising from the ashes. Alongside is Derby County FC's new stadium. To the south, Alvaston Park has an attractive lake and a trail featuring 25 exotic trees. At the end of this section Elvaston Castle which, despite its name, is actually a country house, is set in more than 200 acres (81ha) of woodland, parkland and formal gardens with picnic tables, play areas, nature trails and tearooms.

The Riverside Gardens are a few yards north of the bus station. Here, by the stepped riverbank with its Canada geese, the Way passes through Derby city centre. The path passes under a modern road bridge and continues along the river, signposted to Melbourne and Little Eaton. To the right lie the grassy hummocks of Bass's Recreation Ground, shown on the OS map as The Holmes.

Continue, and take the footbridge with white railings that lies ahead and crosses a quiet water channel. Follow the path round to a red metal fingerpost. Along here the Derwent Valley Heritage Way coincides with the National Cycle Network which means there's a very good quality surface to the path.

≷ ⊞ 🅿 To reach the railway station from here, go right under the flyover and along Railway Terrace for 300 yds (273m), noting the unusual fence by the car park with railway paraphernalia built into its design. The clock on the adjacent Wyvern House is also worth a glance. If you are starting this section of the route from the railway station, simply reverse the above instructions to reach the riverside path.

🅐 Continue ahead, passing under a low structure known as Five Arches Bridge, to follow the obvious path marked with frequent red metal signs and lamp-posts. Shortly, there is a sports centre on the right with an undulating roof. On the left are a couple of rusted vertical metal pillars; these are a sculpture called *Bloodlines*, made from recycled cast-iron rails taken from the Roundhouse, a former railway workshop on Pride Park.

An information board at a paved seating area indicates a few of the

Weir near the Riverside Gardens, Derby

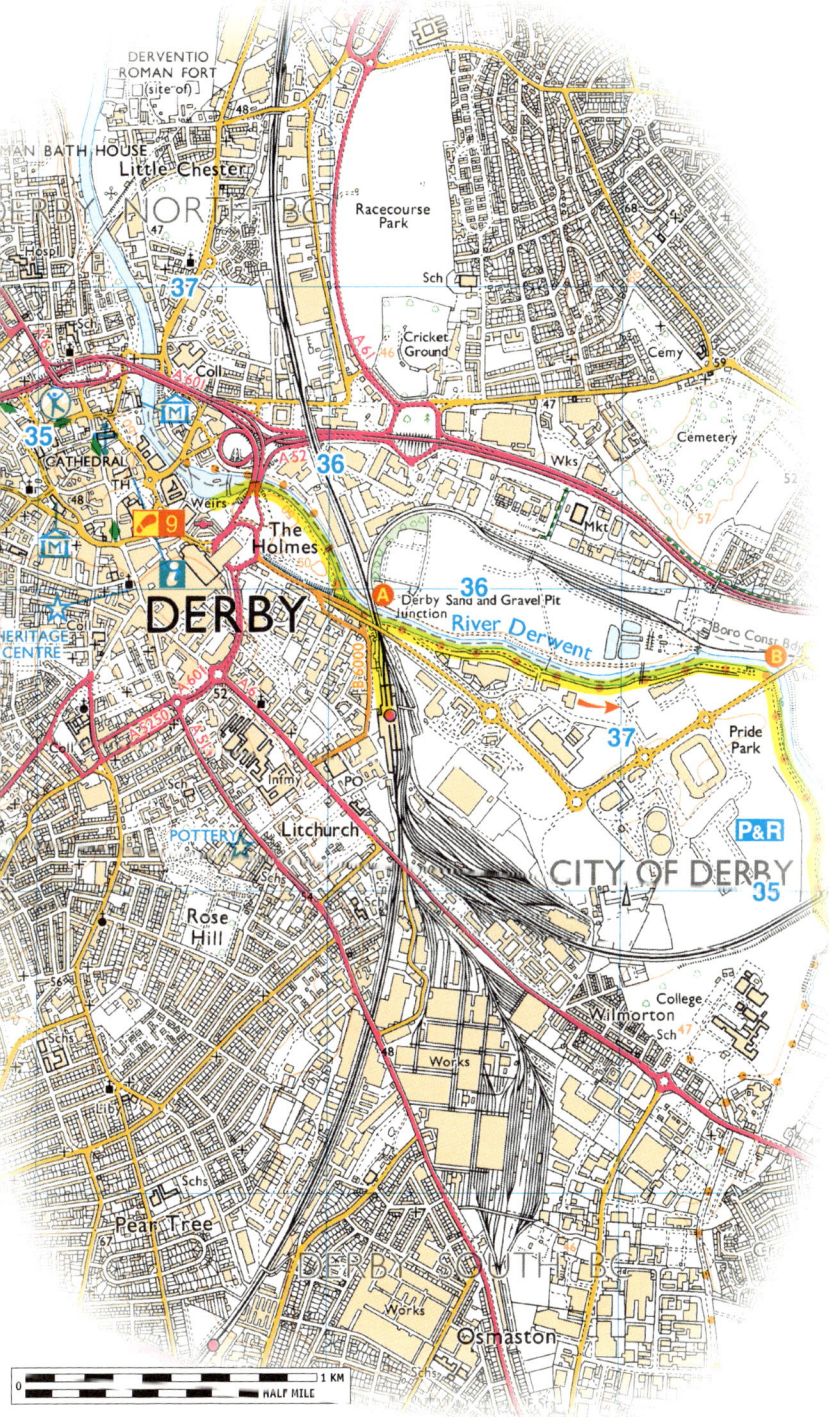

The Pride Park area was the original site of Derby's railway manufacturing industry. Having once employed nearly 6,000 people, by the early 1990s it was derelict. Derby City Partnership began to regenerate the area with £37.5 million from the Government. Many new industrial and commercial units have appeared in the area and among them rises the futuristic outline of Derby County FC's Pride Park Stadium.

species of plants along the river. Most of the trees are crack willows and alders. The smaller plants include comfrey, tansy, butterbur and unwelcome invaders like Himalayan balsam.

B Go under the low modern sweep of the A52 road bridge, continuing as the river swings south to pass below a railway bridge. Just beyond here is one of the 1,000 mileposts erected to mark the creation of the National Cycle Network. To the south, is Alvaston Park with its attractive lake and a tree trail for those of an arboreal disposition.

A National Cycle Network routepost on the Way near Alvaston

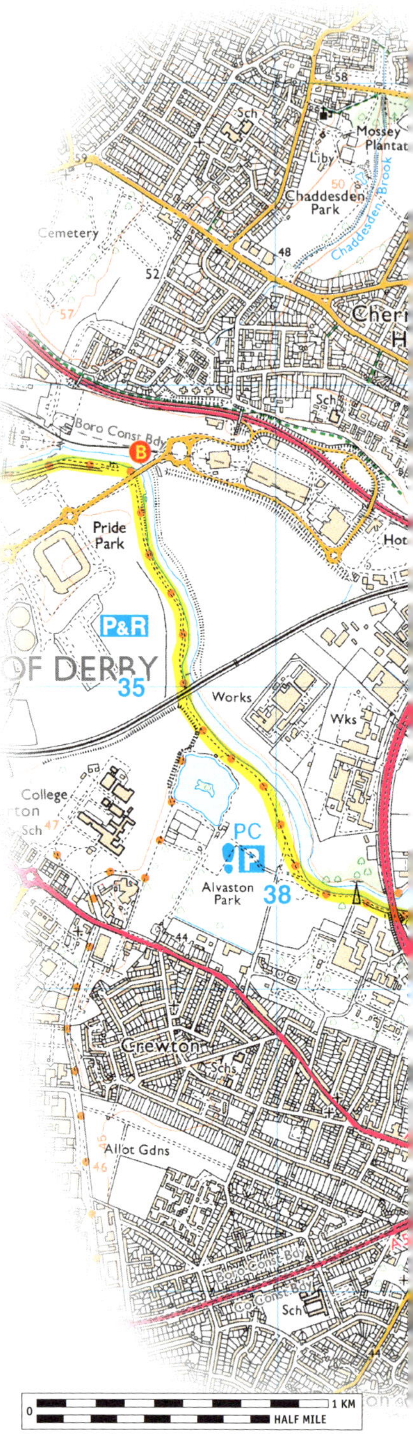

The riverside path continues, with the occasional angler on the left and a hummocky BMX track and a series of sports pitches on the right. Just after a telecommunications mast the Way dips under another bridge, where the path surface changes from tarmac to chippings. Opposite, a channel of the river flows off as a huge meander.

Watch out for a shallow weir a little farther on, seen through railings on the left. This is the Derwent Flood Barrier and just beyond it the meander, which encloses a sizeable island, rejoins the main river channel. Across the flood meadow to the south the tower of St Michael and All Angels Church rises above the houses of Alvaston. Ahead a series of green sluice gates are visible.

C The green barrier, known as Spondon Sluices, was built after a disastrous flood in Derby in 1932. Another meander loops round to the north at this point. It is owned by Acordis, formerly British Celanese, and since 1987 the island in the meander has been run as a private nature reserve. Listen for the chortling calls of green woodpeckers and watch for cormorants flying in this area. The pylon just beyond the sluices seems to be a favourite roost for the local cormorants.

> ■ The Tree Trail in Alvaston Park begins and ends at the car park off Meadow Lane but it can be joined at other points with the very clear map in the leaflet available from Derby City Council. The Tree Trail offers attractive views of the lake and it visits 25 exotic trees, including tree of heaven, honey locust, tulip tree and ornamental pear, as well as the more common beech and oak.

Elvaston Castle in Elvaston Castle Country Park

■ Elvaston Castle, which despite its name is a country house, dates from the early 19th century, having replaced an earlier manor house. For 300 years the Stanhope family lived here. In 1970, Elvaston Castle and its grounds opened as the first country park in Britain. There are more than 200 acres (81ha) of woodland, parkland and formal gardens to explore, plus picnic tables, play areas, nature trails and tearooms.

Beyond another weir the path takes to a levee as far as a concrete bridge. A newly created bridleway from close to the weir leads the short distance to Elvaston Castle Country Park.

D Immediately before the bridge is another of the National Cycle Network mileposts. From here the Way follows a track round to the right. This soon leads to the B5010, also known as Borrowash Lane. Take the footpath to the left along the road as far as Borrowash Bridge.

≋ 🚌 🅿 For buses back to Derby, continue over the bridge and follow Station Road for 600 yds (546m) into the centre of Borrowash. ■

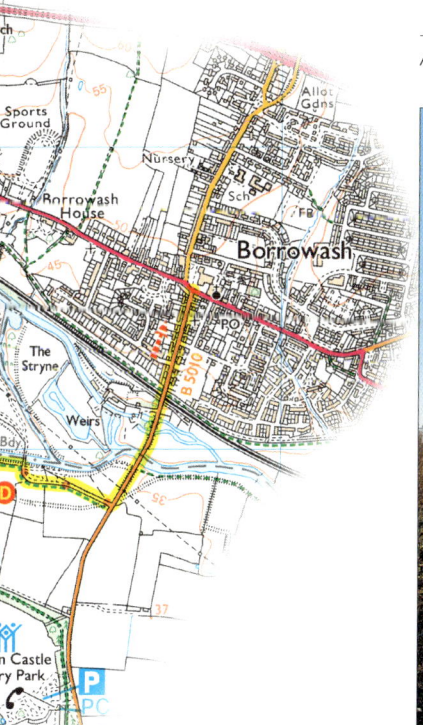

A millennium waymark near Borrowash Bridge

SECTION 10

Borrowash Bridge to Derwent Mouth

START	**Borrowash Bridge/Borrowash centre**
FINISH	**Derwent Mouth**
DISTANCE	**4.6 miles (7.4km)/5.0 miles (8.2km) plus 1 mile (1.6km) return to Shardlow.**
TERRAIN	**Riverside path, minor road, footway, canal towpath**

PUBLIC TRANSPORT

To the start at Borrowash, buses from Derby and Nottingham. From the finish at Shardlow, buses to Derby, Loughborough and Leicester

FACILITIES EN ROUTE

Melbourne

Pubs, restaurants, cafés/tearooms, hotels, B&Bs/guest-houses, banks, shops, public toilets, PO, children's play areas and historical places of interest. Campsites at Hill Farm, Barrow-on-Trent (approximately 4 miles); Shardlow Marina, Shardlow (approximately 6 miles) and two at Elvaston (Elvaston Castle Caravan Park) and Beechwood Park (approximately 5 miles)

Shardlow

Pubs, restaurants, tearooms, hotels, B&Bs/guest-houses, shops, PO, historical places of interest. Camp sites at Shardlow Marina, Shardlow and two at Elvaston (Elvaston Castle Caravan Park) and Beechwood Park (approximately 5 miles) Hill Farm, Barrow-on-Trent (approximately 6 miles)

Ambaston

Nearest pub is in Thulston (1.3 miles), restaurants and shops in Borrowash and Shardlow 1.5 miles. Campsites at Shardlow Marina, Shardlow (1.5 miles), two at Elvaston (Elvaston Castle Caravan Park) and Beechwood Park (approximately 1.5 miles) Hill Farm, Barrow-on-Trent (approximately 7 miles)

Heatherdene
1

Leadmill Bridge
2

Baslow
3

Rowsley
4

Matlock
5

Whatstandwell
6

Belper
7

Little Eaton
8

Derby City Centre
9

Borrowash Bridge
10

Derwent Mouth

The Trent and Mersey Canal at Shardlow

The final section of the Way follows fields to Ambaston. A minor road then leads to Shardlow, an intriguing old inland port from where a towpath leads to a triple confluence of the Trent and Mersey Canal with the Rivers Derwent and Trent.

Shardlow, a prime port until the development of the railways led to the decline of the waterways, was designated a Conservation Area in 1974. There is much to investigate, including the Clock Warehouse, now a family pub, and the Heritage Centre, run by volunteers and the source of many fascinating facts.

SECTION TEN

Borrowash Bridge to Derwent Mouth

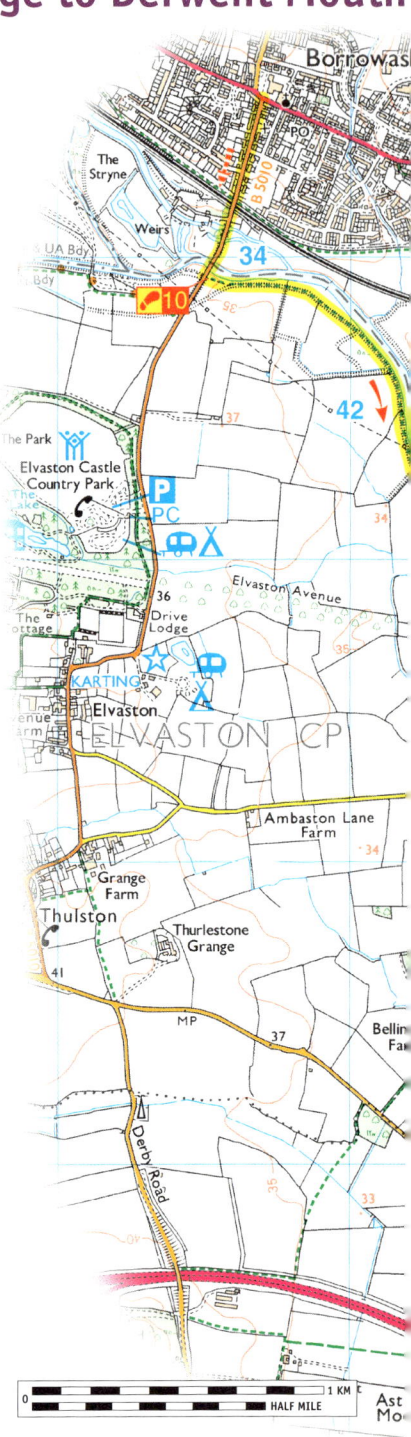

≈ 🚌 From bus stops in the centre of Borrowash follow Station Road for 600 yds (546m) to reach Borrowash Bridge.

From the southern side of Borrowash Bridge take the steps down, alongside the 30mph sign with a DVHW waymark. From here a field path follows a low levee eastwards. Looking back, you can see the bridge has extra arches over either bank to accommodate floodwater. The path briefly angles away from the riverbank before coming back alongside it. This is a quiet stretch of walking, particularly after the river loops away from the busy main railway line which runs to the south of Borrowash village. Continue as far as a narrow strip of recently planted trees where a waymark points to the right down newly-made steps.

Ⓐ Immediately beyond the trees the path goes half left across fields with a series of stiles well marked to show the way. The path becomes a grassy track which enters Ambaston and turns right into Main Street, the village's only road.

Follow this through Ambaston and then southwards as a quiet minor road called Ambaston Lane, mainly between hedges, towards Shardlow. A few miles away to the east the clustered cooling towers of the power station at Ratcliffe on Soar are prominent.

Ⓑ On reaching Shardlow turn left on the footway alongside London Road and walk through the scattered village, passing Shardlow Hall, to the most interesting part of Shardlow

Narrowboats on the Trent and Mersey Canal, Shardlow

■ Shardlow was an important inland port, close to the point where the Trent and Mersey Canal joined the River Trent. After the canal opened fully in 1777 Shardlow grew rapidly to a population of 1,300 in 1841. By then railway development was leading to the decline of the waterways. In 1974 the port area of Shardlow was designated a Conservation Area. There is much to see, not least the Clock Warehouse, now a family pub which nevertheless retains its bold lettering 'NAVIGATION FROM the TRENT to the MERSEY' and the date '1780'. Adjacent is the Heritage Centre, run by volunteers and a source of fascinating information.

half a mile (805m) to the east. Cross the bridge over the canal opposite the Heritage Centre, noting its weathervane featuring a narrowboat, then immediately turn left between white fences to reach the towpath.

C The next stretch of the route passes narrowboat moorings, canalside pubs, cottages and converted warehouses. This makes for easy and very attractive walking. Pass under another bridge beyond which are more narrowboats and the Chapel Farm Marina on the opposite side of the canal. A plaque on Porter's Bridge indicates that it is the first bridge on the canal. Soon after this is a small weir by Derwent Mouth Lock, just 98ft (30m) above sea level.

D Beyond this stretch, both the Derwent and Trent can swell after heavy rain and flood the final 300 yds (273m) of the Way. Normally the towpath is easily passable and it soon reaches Long Horse Bridge. This footbridge over the Trent is closed at the time of writing but there are

hopes that it will reopen in 2004. It also marks the confluence of three important waterways: the Trent and Mersey Canal, the River Trent and the River Derwent. Thus it is also the end of an intriguing walk through the heart of Derbyshire, the 55-mile (88.5km) Derwent Valley Heritage Way.

≈ 🚌 🅿 From here retrace your steps for the mile (1.6 km) back to Shardlow from where there are buses to Derby, Loughborough and Leicester. ■

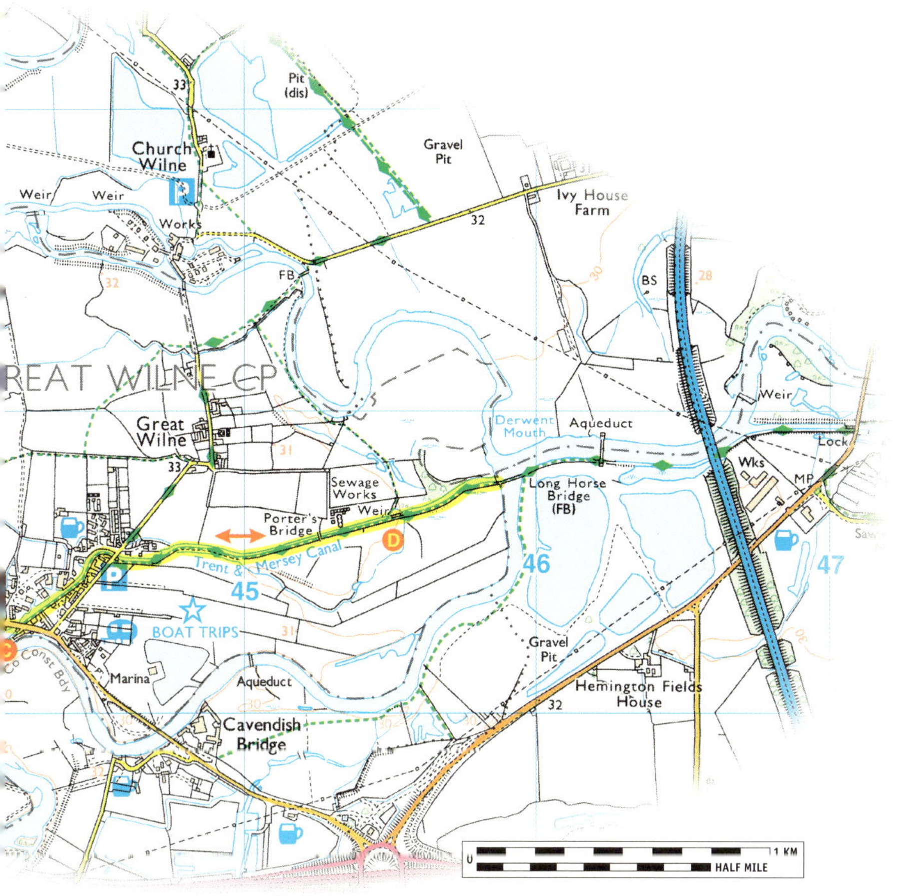

Long Horse Bridge, the southern end of the Derwent Valley Heritage Way

Further Information

The Derwent Valley Trust

The Derwent Valley Trust is a charitable trust supported by all the local authorities and many other organisations and businesses in this part of Derbyshire. It was established to secure recognition of the River Derwent and its immediate corridor for its landscape, wildlife and heritage. The Trust is keen not only to promote the Derwent Valley and its attractions but to encourage visitors to protect the area by using their cars less – by walking, cycling and using public transport.

Financial support for the creation of the Derwent Valley Heritage Way came from Lafarge Cement, Derbyshire County Council, Peak District National Park Authority, East Midlands Development Agency, the Environment Agency, Southern Derbyshire Chamber and WREN (Waste Recycling Environmental) through tax credits. Other agencies supported the provision of interpretative panels along the route and various voluntary agencies helped with work on the ground. A Heritage Way steering group, including Dr Brian Waters, chair of the Derwent Valley Trust, was established and Rick Jillings, based in Derbyshire County Council's Countryside Service, was appointed as Project Officer. His brief was to bring the idea of the Derwent Valley Heritage Way to fruition.

You could assist the Trust to promote the Derwent Valley, the Heritage Way and other projects. Please consider a donation to: Derwent Valley Trust, c/o Robinsons Solicitors, 83 Friars Gate, Derby, DE1 1FL. A Gift Aid form can be requested from the trust website. You will also find information on the Derwent Valley Trust and the Heritage Way at:
www.nationalheritagecorridor.org.uk

Places to explore

The main text gives details of many places worthy of a visit. Those with formal entrance arrangements, which are on, or close to, the Derwent Valley Heritage Way, are listed here in (approximate) north to south order:

Hathersage Open-Air Heated Swimming Pool.
Tel: 01433 650843.
Open Easter–Oct. Call for times. Admission charge.

David Mellor Cutlery Factory and Country Shop, Hathersage.
Tel: 01433 650220.
www.davidmellordesign.co.uk
Shop open all year. Call for times and details of factory visits.

Chatsworth House and Gardens, Bakewell. Tel: 01246 582204.
www.chatsworth.org.
House open from Apr–Dec. Call for times. Admission charges to house, gardens, farmyard and adventure playground.

Haddon Hall, Bakewell.
Tel: 01629 812855.
www.haddonhall.co.uk
Open from Apr–end Sept. Call for times. Admission charge.

Shardlow Heritage Centre

Caudwell's Mill and Craft Centre, Rowsley. Tel: 01629 734374.
www.information-britain.co.uk
Open 9.30 am–5.30 pm all year. Entry to craft workshops, shops and café free. Admission charge to mill.

Peak Rail, Matlock.
(Runs steam rail services between Matlock Riverside and Rowsley South.) Tel: 01629 580381.
www.peakrail.co.uk
Call for details of timetables and fares.

Red House Working Carriage Museum, Darley Dale.
Tel: 01629 733583.
Open all year. Call for times.

The Whistlestop Centre (Derbyshire Wildlife Trust), Matlock Bath.
Tel: 01629 580958.
www.derbyshirewildlifetrust.org.uk
Open 10 am–5 pm Apr–Oct,
12 noon–4 pm weekends only
Nov–Mar. Admission free.

Peak District Mining Museum and Temple Mine, Matlock Bath.
Tel: 01629 583834.
www.peakmines.co.uk

Museum open all year, Temple Mine open weekends only in winter. Call for times. Admission charge.

Gulliver's Kingdom, Matlock Bath.
('Fun-land' attractions.) Tel: 01629 580540. Opening times vary.

The Heights of Abraham, Matlock Bath. (Family attraction, including cable cars and show caverns).
Tel: 01629 582365.
www.heights-of-abraham.co.uk
Open seasonally. Admission charge. Call for details.

Masson Mills (Working Textile Museum), Matlock Bath.
Tel: 01629 581001.
www.massonmills.co.uk
Open all year. Call for times.

Cromford Mill.
Tel: 01629 823256.
www.cromfordmill.co.uk
Open 9am–5 pm all year.

Willersley Castle, Cromford.
(Operated as a hotel by Christian Guild Holidays). Tel: 01629 582270.
www.cgholidays.co.uk
Open 9.30 am–6 pm all year.

High Peak Junction Workshops, Cromford. Tel: 01629 822831 or 823204.
www.derbyshire.gov. uk/countryside
Open daily in summer
10.30 am–5.30 pm, weekends in winter 10.30 am–4 pm.

National Stone Centre, Wirksworth. Tel: 01629 824833.
www.nationalstonecentre.org.uk
Open all year. Call for times.

Leawood Pumphouse, Cromford.
Tel: 01629 823204.
www.derbyshire.gov.uk/countryside
Opening times vary. Admission free.

Crich Tramway Village.
Tel: 01773 852326.
www.tramway.co.uk
Open all year. Call for times.
Admission charge.

Heage Windmill.
Tel: 01773 606956 or 856467.
Open seasonally. Call for details.

Belper North Mill (Derwent Valley Visitor Centre). Tel: 01773 880474.
www.belpernorthmill.org.uk
Open 1–5 pm all year. Admission charge to mill.

Derby Industrial Museum (Silk Mill) Tel: 01332 255308.
www.derby.gov.uk./museums Open all year. Call for times.

Elvaston Castle and Country Park. Tel: 01332 571342.
www.gardenvisit.com/g/elv.htm
Park open dawn to dusk, all year.

Shardlow Heritage Centre.
Tel: 01332 793368 or 792334 or 792489. Staffed entirely by volunteers. Open seasonally. Admission free. Call for details.

Travel information

The Derwent Valley is easy to get to and travel around. This makes it easy to do a linear walk, say one or two sections of the Way, then return by bus or train.

Rail Services
Tel: 08457 48 49 50
www.nationalrail.co.uk

The Hope Valley line serves the northern section of the Derwent Valley. There are regular trains from Manchester and Sheffield that call at Bamford, Hathersage and Grindleford. Derby is well served by the national rail network. From Derby there are regular services to Matlock calling at Duffield, Belper, Ambergate, Whatstandwell, Cromford and Matlock Bath.

Bus Services TRAVELINE
Tel: 0870 608 2 608
www.traveline.org.uk

There are regular direct bus services to and from Sheffield, Chesterfield, Manchester, Nottingham and Derby. Regular services link to Heatherdene, Bamford, Hathersage, Grindleford, Calver, Baslow and Bakewell. Buses also serve Rowsley, Darley Dale, Matlock, Cromford, Whatstandwell, Ambergate, Belper, Duffield, Little Eaton, Derby, Elvaston, Borrowash and Shardlow.

For up-to-date public transport information in Derbyshire visit www.derbysbus.net For full public transport information the Peak District and Mid and South

Derbyshire timetables are available from Tourist Information Centres (60p at the time of writing) or by post from Derbyshire County Council Public Transport Unit, County Hall, Matlock DE4 3AG (£1.20 inc. postage). Having used both publications as I researched this book, I can recommend them.

Sources of information

Tourist Information Centres
Old Market Hall, Bridge Street, Bakewell
Tel: 01629 813227

The Pavilion, Matlock Bath
Tel: 01629 55082

Assembly Rooms, Market Place, Derby
Tel: 01332 255802

Crown Square, Matlock
Tel: 01629 583388

Town Hall, Market Place, Ripley
Tel: 01773 841488

The Crescent, Buxton,
Tel: 01298 25106

Other sources of information
Derwent Valley Visitor Centre, Belper North Mill, Bridgefoot, Belper
Tel: 01773 880474

Derbyshire Countryside Service, Middleton Top Visitor Centre, Middleton-by-Wirksworth
Tel: 01629 823204

Upper Derwent Information Centre, Fairholmes, Nr. Bamford
Tel: 01433 650953

Derbyshire Countryside Service
Elvaston Castle Country Park
Borrowash Road, Elvaston
Tel: 01332 571342

Sir Richard Arkwright's Cromford Mill, Mill Lane, Cromford
Tel: 01629 823256

Shardlow Heritage Centre
London Road, Shardlow
Tel: 01332 793368 or 792334

Peak District Mining Museum
The Pavilion, Matlock Bath
Tel: 01629 583834

Derbyshire Wildlife Trust
Whistlestop Countryside Centre
The Railway Station
Tel: 01629 580958

The Upper Derwent Valley

The Derwent Valley Heritage Way begins at Heatherdene, close to the southern end of Ladybower Reservoir. North lies the Upper Derwent Valley, which already attracts many thousands of visitors each year. For this reason the Derwent Valley Heritage Way has not been formally extended into the Upper Derwent Valley but, with increasingly good public transport services, it is easy to explore the upper reaches of the Derwent without putting additional pressure on the road network.

Calver Mill

That crowds are attracted to the Upper Derwent is not surprising, given its easy accessibility via the A57 and its spectacular scenery. The Howden, Derwent and Ladybower reservoirs, three stretches of blue on fine days, lie cradled below the high moors. From Derwent Edge a series of unusual rock tors – the Salt Cellar, the Cakes of Bread, the Wheel Stones – look down on the upper reaches of the river and the reservoirs it fills.

Walking and cycling are ideal ways to explore the valley and get close to its wildlife. Common sandpipers nest on the stony edges of the reservoirs. Red-breasted mergansers are not uncommon in the breeding season. The occasional goshawk or buzzard may be seen, usually near the plantations and woods. Following the infant Derwent north from King's Tree, past the bridge at Slippery Stones, may well bring sightings of grey wagtails and dippers.

For those properly equipped and confident with map and compass, exploring the moorland where the Derwent begins adds an extra dimension to an appreciation of the river. The vegetation is mainly heather, bilberry, cotton grass and purple moor grass. This is the territory of red grouse and merlin. In summer, curlews may well be heard, the occasional dunlin may be spotted and, with their recent re-colonisation of the Peak, there is an increasing chance of seeing ravens. In sheltered cloughs on the moorland fringes the green hairstreak butterfly may catch the eye.

Exploring the headwaters of the Derwent provides superb walking when weather conditions are good. There are expansive views and the chance for a close look at some of the rock outcrops – Grinah Stones maybe, or the Rocking Stone on Outer Edge.

It is these attractions, and the scope for more easily accessible and less strenuous activities in the valley, which draw the crowds. With just a narrow cul-de-sac road running for the few miles from the A57, along the western side of the three reservoirs in the valley, there is major traffic pressure, particularly at weekends in summer.

Consequently, in an attempt to manage the Upper Derwent Valley for the benefit of all concerned, a traffic management scheme is in operation at certain times. On summer Sundays and Bank Holidays the road is closed to traffic north of Fairholmes, which has parking, an information centre, refreshments, toilets and cycle hire. A shuttle minibus serves the valley north of Fairholmes at these times.

In addition, Derbyshire County Council has announced its intention to introduce a toll scheme on the Fairholmes road as a further traffic management strategy. With bus services running to Fairholmes from Manchester, Sheffield, Bakewell and Buxton, using public transport and walking is the greenest way to reach the Upper Derwent Valley.

Access for all

The Derwent Valley Heritage Way follows field and woodland paths, tracks and sections of pavement and road. Although it basically follows a valley, there are some climbs and descents, most notably in Section 5, though there is a low-level alternative here. The terrain generally makes for easy walking, but some stretches can be wet underfoot and prone to flooding.

Within the Peak District National Park many stiles have been replaced with gates to make access easier. The National Park produces a free Access For All Guide (01629 816200). Sections of the Derwent Valley Heritage Way that are accessible by wheelchair include Ladybower Dam, the Thornhill Trail, Matlock Parks including Hall Leys and Lovers Walk in Matlock Bath, and the Cromford Canal from Cromford to High Peak Junction.

In addition, wheelchairs are welcome where the Way coincides with Route 54 of the National Cycle Network from Little Eaton, linking with the cycle route through Darley Playing Fields into Derby city centre, and on Route 6, where the Riverside Path coincides with the Derwent Valley Heritage Way from Derby city centre as far as Borrowash.

The DVHW walk recorder

Mike Warner, of the Long Distance Walkers' Association, has volunteered to act as the DVHW Walk Recorder. If you would like to record your achievement in this way, a pack, including a certificate and badge, is available from Mike with a small charge. Please enclose a cheque for £5 made payable to the Derwent Valley Trust and Heritage Way. Write to: Mike Warner, Derwent Valley Heritage Way Recorder, Redland House, Clifton, Ashbourne, Derbyshire DE6 2GJ.

www.totalwalking.co.uk

www.totalwalking.co.uk
is the official website of the Jarrold
Pathfinder and Short Walks guides. This
interactive website features a wealth of
information for walkers – from the latest
news on route diversions and advice from
professional walkers to product news, free
sample walks and promotional offers.

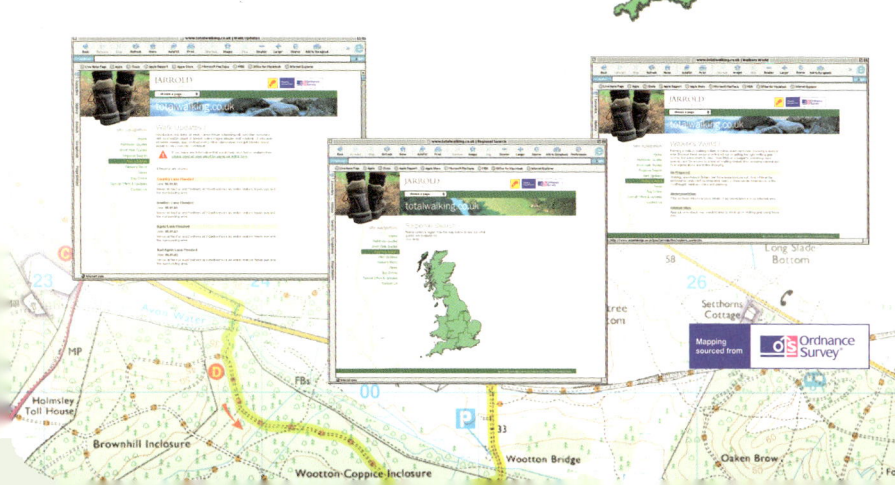